Crocheted Houseplants

Crocheted Houseplants

BEAUTIFUL FLORA TO MAKE FOR YOUR HOME

EMMA VARNAM

Contents

Introduction

When I wrote *Crocheted Succulents*, my first plant book, I never imagined how much fun and enjoyment these little projects would give me and my friends in the crafting community. I have seen my patterns made all over the world, including Australia, South Korea, South America and Europe.

Many people have displayed their real plants alongside their crocheted creations. Often there is a double take before people realise that a woolly specimen is sitting incognito among the genuine ones.

Houseplants have seen a fashionable resurgence in recent years. Chic interiors have been enhanced by elegant palms, huge Swiss cheese plants and glorious draping vines.

I enjoy gardening and I also enjoy having houseplants in our home; a combination of succulents and leafy plants. Some have survived many years, others I have unceremoniously killed through overwatering or neglectful drought. Luckily, using crochet, you can make a plant that is impossible to kill. Crocheted plants are still one of my favourite choices for giving

as gifts and, by writing this book, I have added to my go-to list for hand-made presents. I had such fun making these patterns. You should feel sorry for my poor family and friends, who were sent endless photos with the caption, 'isn't this hilarious?' whenever I came up with a new idea.

One thing to be aware of is that leafy plants with stems made from wool cannot defy gravity. Therefore, all the plants in this book have been made to fit posts of 2¼–4¾in (6–12cm). I have made them a modest size and have stiffened their stems using plant stakes and wire. If you want to make a 36in (1m)-high Swiss cheese plant, you will need to double up your yarn thickness and have a very robust plant stake for support. It is possible, but make sure it is stable and safe.

I must confess I have found it difficult to part with the finished products. I have mixed them in with my living plant collection on our mantlepiece, and it is often difficult to tell them apart.

LEFT TO RIGHT:
SNAKE PLANT, PAGE 28
BOSTON FERN, PAGE 98
CENTURY PLANT, PAGE 60
TIGER ALOE, PAGE 32

LEFT TO RIGHT:
POINSETTIA, PAGE 90
HERRINGBONE PLANT, PAGE 86

SPIDER PLANT, PAGE 20

Saintpaulia ionantha

African Violet

This is a pretty plant with vibrant flowers. People often over-water the living version, but you won't need to worry about that with the crocheted alternative. By combining wool with a soft mohair yarn you can recreate the lovely fluffy texture of the leaves.

FINISHED SIZE

The longest strands are approximately 4¾in (12cm) wide.

YOU WILL NEED

- Scheepjes Metropolis, 75% wool, 25% nylon (219yd/200m per 50g ball): 1 ball in 031 Canberra (A), 026 Depok (B) and 053 Santiago (C)
- Scheepjes Mohair Rhythm, 30% microfibre, 70% mohair (219yd/200m per 25g ball): 1 ball in 678 Boogie (D)
- Sirdar Happy Cotton, 100% cotton (47yd/43m per 20g ball): Small amount of 788 Quack (E)
- Scheepjes Merino Soft, 50% wool, 25% microfibre, 25% acrylic (115yd/105m per 50g ball): 1 ball in 607 Braque (F)
- 3.5mm (UK9:USE/4) crochet hook
- Polyester stuffing
- Tapestry needle
- Plant pot approximately 2¾in (6cm) in diameter

TENSION

Tension is not essential for this project.

Note

Create the soft and slightly hairy leaves by working a soft mohair yarn together with your choice of main colour for the leaves.

Leaf
(make 16)

Make 8 using A and D together and 8 using B and D together.
Using 3.5mm hook ch 8.

Row 1: 1 dc in 2nd ch, 1 htr, 1 tr, (2 tr in next ch), 1 tr, 1 htr, 1 dc in last ch, 2 ch, (now turn and work down the other side of the foundation ch), 1 dc, 1 htr, 1 tr, (2 tr in next ch), 1 tr, 1 htr, 1 dc, 1 sl st in first ch.

Fasten off and leave a tail of yarn.

Flower
(make 3)

Using 3.5mm hook and C, make a magic ring (see page 129).

Round 1: 1 ch, 5 dc into the centre of the ring, join with a sl st.

Round 2: (6 ch, 3 tr, 6 ch, sl st) in first st, * sl st in next st, (6 ch, 3 tr, 6 ch, sl st) in same st; rep from * 3 times.

Fasten off and leave a yarn tail.

Using yarn E and a tapestry needle make two small French knots in the centre of the flower.

Soil

Using 3.5mm hook and F, make a magic ring.

Round 1: 1 ch, 6 dc into the centre of the ring.

Round 2: 2 dc into each st (12 sts).

Round 3: (1 dc, dc2inc) 6 times (18 sts).

Round 4: (2 dc, dc2inc) 6 times (24 sts).

Round 5: (3 dc, dc2inc) 6 times (30 sts).

Round 6: (4 dc, dc2inc) 6 times (36 sts).

Round 7: (5 dc, dc2inc) 6 times (42 sts).

Round 8: (6 dc, dc2inc) 6 times (48 sts).

Rounds 9–16: Work 8 rounds straight.

Round 17: (6 dc, dc2tog) 6 times (42 sts).

Round 18: (5 dc, dc2tog) 6 times (36 sts).

Round 19: (4 dc, dc2tog) 6 times (30 sts).

Round 20: (3 dc, dc2tog) 6 times (24 sts).

Round 21: (2 dc, dc2tog) 6 times (18 sts).

Stuff firmly with polyester stuffing.

Round 22: (1 dc, dc2tog) 6 times (12 sts).

Round 23: (Dc2tog) 6 times (6 sts).

Using a tapestry needle, weave this yarn through the last dc sts of the round and gather hole together. Fasten off and weave in ends.

Making up

Arrange eight lighter green leaves in a star on the top of the soil. Sew firmly in place. Then place the eight darker leaves in the spaces between the lighter leaves to create an overlapping star. Sew those firmly in place. Now sew the three flowers together in the centre of the plant.

Chlorophytum comosum

Spider Plant

This is one of the most popular houseplants for two reasons: it appears to be almost indestructible, and it has little offshoot babies that grow at the end of long stems. The attractive crochet version looks great in a hanging pot.

FINISHED SIZE

The plant in its pot is approximately 10in (25cm) tall and 10in (25cm) wide.

TENSION

Tension is not essential for this project.

YOU WILL NEED

- Scheepjes Metropolis, 75% wool, 25% nylon (219yd/200m per 50g ball): 1 ball in 033 Atlanta (A) 031 Canberra (B) and 032 Abu Dhabi (C)
- Scheepjes Merino Soft, 50% wool, 25% microfibre, 25% acrylic (115yd/105m per 50g ball): 1 ball in 607 Braque (D)
- 3mm (UK11:US–) crochet hook
- 3.5mm (UK9:USE/4) crochet hook
- Polyester stuffing
- Tapestry needle
- Floristry wire
- Plant pot approximately 4in (10cm) in diameter

Note

The plant leaves are worked in rows. Create strength in the leaf by working around a wire on row 2 (see page 133). Work one side of the leaf, then the other side, and then complete the leaf by working a final row of dc in yarn B or C.

Large leaf
(make 3)

Row 1: Using 3mm hook and A, ch 37 sts. Hold your floristry wire above your ch sts; you will work around the wire to encase it in the crochet.

Row 2: Insert your hook into the 2nd st from the hook, yarn over the hook, pull through the stitch, put your hook over the wire and the stitches and wrap the yarn over the hook and pull through both loops on the hook, encasing the wire. Rep to the end of the ch stitches, pm, turn (36 sts).

Pull the wire so that it is at the beginning of the row.

Row 3 WS: Ch 1, 33 dc, 3 sl st, 1 ch, (now work down the other side of the leaf into the other side of the ch sts), 3 sl st, 33 dc, turn (73 sts).

Fasten off yarn A and leave a long tail of yarn.

Row 4 RS: Change to yarn B, 1 ch, 33 dc, 3 sl st, (1 sl st, 2 ch, 1 sl st) in ch sp, 3 sl st, 33 dc.

Fasten off and leave a tail of yarn.

Medium leaf
(make 6)

Make 3 using A and B and another 3 using A and C.

Row 1: Using 3mm hook and A, ch 31 sts. Hold your floristry wire above your ch sts; you will work around the wire to encase it in the crochet.

Row 2: Insert your hook into the 2nd st from the hook, yarn over the hook, pull through the stitch, put your hook over the wire and the stitches and wrap the yarn over the hook and pull through both loops on the hook, encasing the wire. Rep to the end of the ch stitches, pm, turn (30 sts).

Pull the wire so that it is at the beginning of the row.

Row 3 WS: Ch 1, 27 dc, 3 sl st, 1 ch, (now work down the other side of the leaf into the other side of the ch sts), 3 sl st, 27 dc, turn (61 sts).

Fasten off yarn A and leave a long tail of yarn.

Row 4 RS: Change to yarn B (or C), 1 ch, 27 dc, 3 sl st, (1 sl st, 2 ch, 1 sl st) in ch sp, 3 sl st, 27 dc.

Fasten off and leave a tail of yarn.

Small leaf
(make 4)

Row 1: Using 3mm hook and A, ch 21 sts. Hold your floristry wire above your ch sts; you will work around the wire to encase it in the crochet.

Row 2: Insert your hook into the 2nd st from the hook, yarn over the hook, pull through the stitch, put your hook over the wire and the stitches and wrap the yarn over the hook and pull through both loops on the hook, encasing the wire. Rep to the end of the ch stitches, pm, turn (20 sts).

Pull the wire so that it is at the beginning of the row.

Row 3 WS: Ch 1, 17 dc, 3 sl st, 1 ch, (now work down the other side of the leaf into the other side of the ch sts), 3 sl st, 17 dc, turn (41 sts).

Fasten off yarn A and leave a long tail of yarn.

Row 4 RS: Change to yarn C, 1 ch, 17 dc, 3 sl st, (1 sl st, 2 ch, 1 sl st) in ch sp, 3 sl st, 17 dc.

Fasten off and leave a tail of yarn.

Long stem

Take a strand of wire and work chain stitches around the wire. Using A and 3mm hook, place a sl st on the hook. With the wire in the hand that holds your yarn, place the yarn under the wire and the hook over the wire, yarn over the hook and pull through the sl st.

Put your hook under the wire and yarn over, pull up, then put your hook over the wire, yarn over, pull through both loops on the hook. Rep until you have 31 sts.

Baby leaf (make 3)

Make 1 using A and 2 using B.
Row 1: Using 3mm hook, ch 17 sts. Hold the floristry wire above your ch sts; you will work around the wire to encase it in the crochet.
Row 2: Insert your hook into the 2nd st from the hook, yarn over the hook, pull through the stitch, put your hook over the wire and the stitches and wrap the yarn over the hook and pull through both loops on the hook, encasing the wire. Rep to the end of the ch stitches, pm, turn (16 sts).
Pull the wire so that it is at the beginning of the row. Cut off the wire to fit the chain stitches. Weave in all ends.

Soil

Using 3.5mm hook and D, make a magic ring (see page 129).
Round 1: 1 ch, 6 dc into the centre of the ring.
Round 2: 2 dc into each st (12 sts).
Round 3: (1 dc, dc2inc) 6 times (18 sts).

Round 4: (2 dc, dc2inc) 6 times (24 sts).
Round 5: (3 dc, dc2inc) 6 times (30 sts).
Round 6: (4 dc, dc2inc) 6 times (36 sts).
Round 7: (5 dc, dc2inc) 6 times (42 sts).
Round 8: (6 dc, dc2inc) 6 times (48 sts).
Rounds 9–16: Work 8 rounds straight.
Round 17: (6 dc, dc2tog) 6 times (42 sts).
Round 18: (5 dc, dc2tog) 6 times (36 sts).
Round 19: (4 dc, dc2tog) 6 times (30 sts).
Round 20: (3 dc, dc2tog) 6 times (24 sts).
Round 21: (2 dc, dc2tog) 6 times (18 sts).
Stuff firmly with polyester stuffing.
Round 22: (1 dc, dc2tog) 6 times (12 sts).
Round 23: (Dc2tog) 6 times (6 sts).
Using a tapestry needle, weave this yarn through the last dc sts of the round and gather hole together. Fasten off and weave in ends.

Making up

Weave in the stray ends of yarn B and C on each leaf. Poke the wire of each leaf into the soil, then use the long tails of yarn A to sew the base of the leaf securely to the top of the soil. Fold each of the baby leaves in half and sew the centre of the leaves to one end of the plant strand. Then sew the plant stem to the soil at the outer edge of the leaf clump. Curl the leaves slightly to create a natural plant shape.

Epiphyllum anguliger

~~~~~~~~~~~~

Fishbone Cactus

This distinctive plant is often hung up high so its draping leaves can hang down. Native to Mexico, it has beautiful fragrant flowers and produces gooseberry-like fruits. Its wavy shape can easily be recreated in crochet and could even be mistaken for the real plant.

FINISHED SIZE

The longest strands are approximately 10in (25cm) long.

TENSION

Tension is not essential for this project.

YOU WILL NEED

- Scheepjes River Washed, 78% cotton 22% acrylic (142yd/130m per 50g ball):
  1 ball in 962 Narmada (A)
- Scheepjes Merino Soft, 50% wool, 25% microfibre, 25% acrylic (115yd/105m per 50g ball):
  1 ball in 607 Braque (B)
- 3.5mm (UK9:USE/4) crochet hook
- Polyester stuffing
- Tapestry needle
- Floristry wire
- Plant pot approximately 4in (10cm) in diameter

Note

The distinctive waves of this plant are created using different-sized stitches, make sure you keep a consistent stitch tension.

Small strand (make 4)

Using 3.5mm hook and A, ch 22 sts.
Row 1: 1 dc in 2nd ch, (1 htr, 1 tr, 1 htr) in next st, *1 dc in next 2 ch sts, (1 dc, 1 htr, 1 tr) in next st, 3 dtr in next st, (1 tr, 1 htr, 1 dc) in next st; rep from * twice, 4 dc, 1 ch, (now turn and work down the other side of the foundation ch), 1 dc, (1 dc, 1 htr, 1 tr) in next st, 3 dtr in next st, (1 tr, 1 htr, 1 dc) in next st, **2 dc, (1 dc, 1 htr, 1 tr) in next st, 3 dtr in next st, (1 tr, 1 htr, 1 dc) in next st; rep from ** once, 2 dc, 3 tr in next st, 3 dc, 1 sl st in final ch.
Fasten off and leave a tail of yarn.

Medium strand (make 6)

Using 3.5mm hook and A, ch 32 sts.
Row 1: 1 dc in 2nd ch, (1 htr, 1 tr, 1 htr) in next st, *1 dc in next 2 ch sts, (1 dc, 1 htr, 1 tr) in next st, 3 dtr in next st, (1 tr, 1 htr, 1 dc) in next st; rep from * 4 times, 4 dc, 1 ch, (now turn and work down the other side of the foundation ch), 1 dc, (1 dc, 1 htr, 1 tr) in next st, 3 dtr in next st, (1 tr, 1 htr, 1 dc) in next st, **2 dc, (1 dc, 1 htr, 1 tr) in next st, 3 dtr in next st, (1 tr, 1 htr, 1 dc) in next st; rep from ** 3 times, 2 dc, 3 tr in next st, 3 dc, 1 sl st in final ch.
Fasten off and leave a tail of yarn.

Soil

Using 3.5mm hook and B, make a magic ring (see page 129).
Round 1: 1 ch, 6 dc into the centre of the ring.
Round 2: 2 dc into each st (12 sts).
Round 3: (1 dc, dc2inc) 6 times (18 sts).
Round 4: (2 dc, dc2inc) 6 times (24 sts).
Round 5: (3 dc, dc2inc) 6 times (30 sts).
Round 6: (4 dc, dc2inc) 6 times (36 sts).
Round 7: (5 dc, dc2inc) 6 times (42 sts).
Round 8: (6 dc, dc2inc) 6 times (48 sts).
Rounds 9–16: Work 8 rounds straight.
Round 17: (6 dc, dc2tog) 6 times (42 sts).
Round 18: (5 dc, dc2tog) 6 times (36 sts).
Round 19: (4 dc, dc2tog) 6 times (30 sts).
Round 20: (3 dc, dc2tog) 6 times (24 sts).
Round 21: (2 dc, dc2tog) 6 times (18 sts).
Stuff firmly with polyester stuffing.
Round 22: (1 dc, dc2tog) 6 times (12 sts).
Round 23: (Dc2tog) 6 times (6 sts).
Using a tapestry needle, weave this yarn through the last dc sts of the round and gather hole together.
Fasten off and weave in ends.

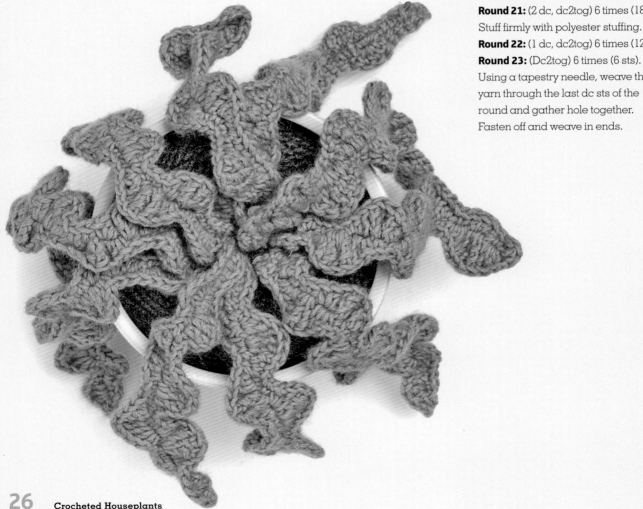

Making up

Weave a strand of floristry
wire through the centre of
the leaves on the wrong side.
Then poke the end of the
floristry wire on each strand
through the soil and fold over
the wire to secure. Sew the
base of the leaf securely to
the top of the soil. Manipulate
the wire to create a natural
plant shape.

Sansevieria trifasciata

Snake Plant

This popular houseplant has helpful air-purifying properties and is sometimes known as mother-in-law's tongue or devil's tongue. Try using a variegated yarn to recreate the natural variations in the markings of this plant.

FINISHED SIZE

The leaves are approximately 10in (25cm) long and 1¾in (4cm) wide.

YOU WILL NEED

- Scheepjes River Washed, 78% cotton, 22% acrylic (142yd/130m per 50g ball): 1 ball in 962 Narmada (A)
- Scheepjes Stone Washed, 78% cotton, 22% acrylic (142yd/130m per 50g ball): 1 ball in 812 Lemon Quartz (B)
- Scheepjes Merino Soft, 50% wool, 25% microfibre, 25% acrylic (115yd/105m per 50g ball): 1 ball in 607 Braque (C)
- 3.5mm (UK9:USE/4) crochet hook
- Tapestry needle
- Pipe cleaners or chenille-covered craft wire
- Bamboo skewer
- Plant pot approximately 4in (10cm) in diameter

TENSION

Tension is not essential for this project.

Note

The plant is worked in rows. Create strength in the leaf by working around a pipe cleaner or chenille wire on row 2. Work one side of the leaf, then the other side and then complete it by working a final row of dc in yarn B. When assembling the plant, use a bamboo skewer to create extra strength at the base.

Leaf (side 1, make 7)

Row 1: Using 3.5mm hook and A, ch 41 sts.
Hold your floristry wire above your ch sts; you will work around the wire to encase it in the crochet.

Row 2: Insert your hook into the 2nd st from the hook, yarn over the hook, pull through the stitch, put your hook over the wire and the stitches and wrap the yarn over the hook and pull through both loops on the hook, encasing the wire. Rep to the end of the ch stitches, pm, turn (40 sts).

Pull the wire so that it is at the beginning of the row.

Row 3 WS: Ch 1, 32 htr, 2 dc, miss 1 st, 1 dc, turn leaving 4 stitches unworked (35 sts).

Row 4 RS: 1 ch, miss 1 st at base of ch, 3 dc, 31 htr.
Fasten off first side of leaf and leave a tail of yarn.

Leaf (side 2, make 7)

You will now work on the second side of the leaf on the other side of the foundation ch. With RS facing, join yarn A with a sl st where you have placed the marker at the base of the leaf.

Row 1 RS: Ch 1, 32 htr, 2 dc, miss 1 st, 1 dc, turn leaving 4 stitches unworked (35 sts).

Row 2 WS: 1 ch, miss 1 st at base of ch, 3 dc, 31 htr, turn.
Fasten off yarn A and join with yarn B.

Edging

You will now work around the edge
of the leaf working over both sides.
Row 1 RS: Ch 1, 40 dc, 2 ch at tip then
work down the second side of the
leaf, 40 dc.
Fasten off and leave a tail of yarn.

Soil

Using 3.5mm hook and C, make a
magic ring (see page 129).
Round 1: 1 ch, 6 dc into the centre of
the ring.
Round 2: 2 dc into each st (12 sts).
Round 3: (1 dc, dc2inc) 6 times (18 sts).
Round 4: (2 dc, dc2inc) 6 times (24 sts).
Round 5: (3 dc, dc2inc) 6 times (30 sts).
Round 6: (4 dc, dc2inc) 6 times (36 sts).
Round 7: (5 dc, dc2inc) 6 times (42 sts).

Round 8: (6 dc, dc2inc) 6 times (48 sts).
Rounds 9–16: Work 8 rounds straight.
Round 17: (6 dc, dc2tog) 6 times (42 sts).
Round 18: (5 dc, dc2tog) 6 times (36 sts).
Round 19: (4 dc, dc2tog) 6 times (30 sts).
Round 20: (3 dc, dc2tog) 6 times (24 sts).
Round 21: (2 dc, dc2tog) 6 times (18 sts).
Stuff firmly with polyester stuffing.
Round 22: (1 dc, dc2tog) 6 times (12 sts).
Round 23: (Dc2tog) 6 times (6 sts).
Using a tapestry needle, weave this
yarn through the last dc sts of the
round and gather hole together. Fasten
off and weave in ends.

Making up

Weave a bamboo skewer
next to the chenille wire
through the centre of the
leaves on the wrong side.
Then poke the end of the
skewer on each leaf through
the soil. Sew the base of the
leaf securely to the top of the
soil. Twist the leaves slightly to
create a natural plant shape.

Gonialoe variegata

Tiger Aloe

Also known as partridge-breasted aloe, the stripy leaf pattern of this South African succulent gives it a distinct identity. This pattern uses a self-striping sock yarn to recreate the stripes without the effort of changing yarns.

FINISHED SIZE

The plant is approximately 4¾in (12cm) tall.

YOU WILL NEED

◆ Opal True Love, 75% wool, 25% polyamide (465yd/425m per 100g ball):
1 ball 9861 in Hakelheld (A)
◆ Scheepjes Merino Soft, 50% wool, 25% microfibre, 25% acrylic (115yd/105m per 50g ball):
1 ball in 607 Braque (B)
◆ 3mm (UK11:US–) crochet hook
◆ 3.5mm (UK9:USE/4) crochet hook
◆ Polyester stuffing
◆ Tapestry needle
◆ Plant pot approximately 4¾in (12cm) in diameter

TENSION

Tension is not essential for this project.

Note

The leaves are worked in spirals using the amigurumi technique (see page 128). Place a marker at the beginning of each round so you know where you are in the pattern.

Leaf
(make 12)

Using 3mm hook and A, make a magic ring (see page 129).

Round 1: 1 ch, 4 dc into the centre of the ring.

Round 2: (1 dc, dc2inc) twice (6 sts).

Rounds 3–5: Work 3 rounds straight.

Round 6: (2 dc, dc2inc) twice (8 sts).

Rounds 7–9: Work 3 rounds straight.

Round 10: (3 dc, dc2inc) twice (10 sts).

Rounds 11–13: Work 3 rounds straight.

Round 14: (4 dc, dc2inc) twice (12 sts).

Rounds 15–17: Work 3 rounds straight.

Round 18: (5 dc, dc2inc) twice (14 sts).

Rounds 19–21: Work 3 rounds straight.

Round 22: (6 dc, dc2inc) twice (16 sts).

Rounds 23–26: Work 4 rounds straight.

Round 27: (7 dc, dc2inc) twice (18 sts).

Rounds 28–31: Work 4 rounds straight. Fasten off and leave a yarn tail.

Soil

Using 3.5mm hook and B, make a magic ring.

Round 1: 1 ch, 6 dc into the centre of the ring.

Round 2: 2 dc into each st (12 sts).

Round 3: (1 dc, dc2inc) 6 times (18 sts).

Round 4: (2 dc, dc2inc) 6 times (24 sts).

Round 5: (3 dc, dc2inc) 6 times (30 sts).

Round 6: (4 dc, dc2inc) 6 times (36 sts).

Round 7: (5 dc, dc2inc) 6 times (42 sts).

Round 8: (6 dc, dc2inc) 6 times (48 sts).

Round 9: (7 dc, dc2inc) 6 times (54 sts).

Round 10: (8 dc, dc2inc) 6 times (60 sts).

Rounds 11–18: Work 8 rounds straight.

Round 19: (8 dc, dc2tog) 6 times (54 sts).

Round 20: (7 dc, dc2tog) 6 times (48 sts).

Round 21: (6 dc, dc2tog) 6 times (42 sts).

Round 22: (5 dc, dc2tog) 6 times (36 sts).

Round 23: (4 dc, dc2tog) 6 times (30 sts).

Round 24: (3 dc, dc2tog) 6 times (24 sts).

Round 25: (2 dc, dc2tog) 6 times (18 sts).

Stuff firmly with polyester stuffing.

Round 26: (1 dc, dc2tog) 6 times (12 sts).

Round 27: (Dc2tog) 6 times (6 sts).

Using a tapestry needle, weave this yarn through the last dc sts of the round and gather hole together. Fasten off and weave in ends.

Making up

Arrange three leaves upright in the middle of the soil and overlap their edges. Pin in place. Then use the tail of the yarn to sew the base of each leaf firmly to the soil. Keep adding a leaf to the outside of these leaves, ensuring that the leaf edges overlap. Sew all the leaves firmly in place.

Cereus peruvianus monstrose

Fairy Castle

This cactus is named after its collection of small turret-like stems. The crocheted version uses small stitches of tinsel yarn applied at the end to create realistic-looking (but non-threatening) spikes.

FINISHED SIZE

The cactus is approximately 3¼in (8cm) tall and 2½in (6cm) wide.

TENSION

Tension is not essential for this project.

YOU WILL NEED

- Scheepjes Metropolis, 75% wool, 25% nylon (219yd/200m per 50g ball): 1 ball in 031 Canberra (A)
- Rico Design Creative Bubble, 100% polyester (98yd/90m per 50g ball): 1 ball in 001 White (B)
- Scheepjes Merino Soft, 50% wool, 25% microfibre, 25% acrylic (115yd/105m per 50g ball): 1 ball in 607 Braque (C)
- 3.5mm (UK9:USE/4) crochet hook
- Polyester stuffing
- Tapestry needle
- Plant pot approximately 4in (10cm) in diameter

Note

The cactus is worked in rows and the spikes are stitched on afterwards. The ridges are formed by working through the back loop only (see page 132).

Large cactus

Row 1: Using 3.5mm hook and A, ch 17 sts.

Row 2 RS: 1 dc in 2nd ch from hook, dc into each ch to end, turn (16 sts).

Rows 3–5: Ch 1, 1 dc in each st to end, turn (16 sts).

Row 6: Ch 1, dc blo into each st to end, turn (16 sts).

Rows 7–9: Ch 1, 1 dc in each st to end, turn (16 sts).

Row 10: Ch 1, dc blo into each st to end, turn (16 sts).

Rows 11–13: Ch 1, 1 dc in each st to end, turn (16 sts).

Rep rows 6–13 three times.

Row 38: Ch 1, dc blo into each st to end, turn (16 sts).

Rows 39–41: Ch 1, 1 dc in each st to end, turn (16 sts).

With RS together, crochet the first and last rows together.

Next row: Ch 1, sl st in every st. Fasten off and leave a long tail.

Medium cactus

Row 1: Using 3.5mm hook and A, ch 13 sts.

Row 2 RS: 1 dc in 2nd ch from hook, dc into each ch to end, turn (12 sts).

Rows 3–5: Ch 1, 1 dc in each st to end, turn (12 sts).

Row 6: Ch 1, dc blo into each st to end, turn (12 sts).

Rows 7–9: Ch 1, 1 dc in each st to end, turn (12 sts).

Row 10: Ch 1, dc blo into each st to end, turn (12 sts).

Rows 11–13: Ch 1, 1 dc in each st to end, turn (12 sts).

Rep rows 6–13 three times.

Row 38: Ch 1, dc blo into each st to end, turn (12 sts).

Rows 39–41: Ch 1, 1 dc in each st to end, turn (12 sts).

With RS together, crochet the first and last rows together.

Next row: Ch 1, sl st in every st. Fasten off and leave a long tail.

Small cactus

Row 1: Using 3.5mm hook and A, ch 9 sts.

Row 2 RS: 1 dc in 2nd ch from hook, dc into each ch to end, turn (8 sts).

Rows 3–5: Ch 1, 1 dc in each st to end, turn (8 sts).

Row 6: Ch 1, dc blo into each st to end, turn (8 sts).

Rows 7–9: Ch 1, 1 dc in each st to end, turn (8 sts).

Row 10: Ch 1, dc blo into each st to end, turn (8 sts).

Rows 11–13: Ch 1, 1 dc in each st to end, turn (8 sts).

Rep rows 6–13 three times.

Row 38: Ch 1, dc blo into each st to end, turn (8 sts).

Rows 39–41: Ch 1, 1 dc in each st to end, turn (8 sts).

With RS together, crochet the first and last rows together.

Next row: Ch 1, sl st in every st. Fasten off and leave a long tail.

Soil

Using 3.5mm hook and C, make a magic ring (see page 129).

Round 1: 1 ch, 6 dc into the centre of the ring.

Round 2: 2 dc into each st (12 sts).

Round 3: (1 dc, dc2inc) 6 times (18 sts).

Round 4: (2 dc, dc2inc) 6 times (24 sts).

Round 5: (3 dc, dc2inc) 6 times (30 sts).

Round 6: (4 dc, dc2inc) 6 times (36 sts).

Round 7: (5 dc, dc2inc) 6 times (42 sts).

Round 8: (6 dc, dc2inc) 6 times (48 sts).

Rounds 9–16: Work 8 rounds straight.

Round 17: (6 dc, dc2tog) 6 times (42 sts).

Round 18: (5 dc, dc2tog) 6 times (36 sts).

Round 19: (4 dc, dc2tog) 6 times (30 sts).

Round 20: (3 dc, dc2tog) 6 times (24 sts).

Round 21: (2 dc, dc2tog) 6 times (18 sts).

Stuff firmly with polyester stuffing.

Round 22: (1 dc, dc2tog) 6 times (12 sts).

Round 23: (Dc2tog) 6 times (6 sts).

Using a tapestry needle, weave this yarn through the last dc sts of the round and gather hole together. Fasten off and weave in ends.

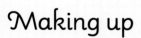
Making up

Each cactus will form into a natural shape of five ridges. With your tapestry needle and a length of yarn, sew small stitches along the top of one side seam to create a star. Firmly stuff the cactus. Take a length of B and your tapestry needle, and over-stitch on the seam evenly to create the spikes. Sew each cactus firmly to the soil.

Moonstones

The unusual egg-shaped leaves give this succulent its Latin name *oviferum*. It also has the common name of sugared almond plant due to the blue-white bloom on its leaves. To achieve a similar effect, find a yarn with a little coloured fleck in its fibres.

FINISHED SIZE

The succulent is approximately 4½in (11cm) in diameter.

TENSION

Tension is not essential for this project.

YOU WILL NEED

- Scheepjes Metropolis, 75% wool, 25% nylon (219yd/200m per 50g ball): 1 ball in 015 Ulsan (A)
- Scheepjes Merino Soft, 50% wool, 25% microfibre, 25% acrylic (115yd/105m per 50g ball): 1 ball in 607 Braque (B)
- 3.5mm (UK9:USE/4) crochet hook
- Polyester stuffing
- Tapestry needle
- Plant pot approximately 3in (7.5cm) in diameter

Note

The succulent is worked in spirals, using the amigurumi technique (see page 128). Place a marker at the beginning of each round so you know where you are in the pattern.

Large leaf
(make 9)

Using 3.5mm hook and A, make a magic ring (see page 129).

Round 1: 1 ch, 5 dc into the centre of the ring.

Round 2: (Dc2inc) 5 times (10 sts).

Round 3: (1 dc, dc2inc) 5 times (15 sts).

Round 4: Work 1 round straight.

Rounds 5: (4 dc, dc2inc) 3 times (18 sts).

Rounds 6–9: Work 4 rounds straight.

Round 10: (4 dc, dc2tog) 3 times (15 sts).

Rounds 11–12: Work 2 rounds straight.

Round 13: (1 dc, dc2tog) 5 times (10 sts). Fasten off and leave a yarn tail.

Small leaf
(make 3)

Using 3.5mm hook and A, make a magic ring.

Round 1: 1 ch, 5 dc into the centre of the ring.

Round 2: (Dc2inc) 5 times (10 sts).

Rounds 3–4: Work 2 rounds straight.

Round 5: (4 dc, dc2inc) twice (12 sts).

Rounds 6–9: Work 4 rounds straight.

Round 10: (4 dc, dc2tog) twice (10 sts). Fasten off and leave a yarn tail.

Centre leaf

Using 3.5mm hook and A, make a magic ring.

Round 1: 1 ch, 5 dc into the centre of the ring.

Round 2: (Dc2inc) 5 times (10 sts).

Rounds 3–7: Work 5 rounds straight.

Round 8: (3 dc, dc2tog) twice (8 sts). Fasten off and leave a yarn tail.

Soil

Using 3.5mm hook and B, make a magic ring.

Round 1: 1 ch, 6 dc into the centre of the ring.

Round 2: 2 dc into each st (12 sts).

Round 3: (1 dc, dc2inc) 6 times (18 sts).

Round 4: (2 dc, dc2inc) 6 times (24 sts).

Rounds 5–12: Work 8 rounds straight.

Round 13: (2 dc, dc2tog) 6 times (18 sts).

Stuff firmly with polyester stuffing.

Round 14: (1 dc, dc2tog) 6 times (12 sts).

Round 15: (Dc2tog) 6 times (6 sts). Using a tapestry needle, weave this yarn through the last dc sts of the round and gather hole together. Fasten off and weave in ends.

Making up

Stuff each leaf with a small amount of polyester stuffing, putting more stuffing at the top of the leaf and leaving less at the base. Arrange six large leaves to form a star and, using the tail of yarn, sew the end rows together to fix the leaves in place. Sew these leaves to your crocheted soil.

Sew another star of three large leaves. Equally space the three small leaves to form a trefoil. Sew these together to ensure their spacing, then sew them on top of your large leaves on the crocheted soil. Finally, sew the small centre leaf right in the middle.

Hoya kerrii

Sweetheart Plant

A popular choice for gifting to a loved one, this slow-growing succulent is also known as a wax heart or sweetheart hoya. It is a robust plant with thick rubbery leaves and is very tolerant if you forget to water it, which is never an issue with the crochet version!

FINISHED SIZE

The cactus is approximately 3¼in (8cm) tall and 3½in (9cm) wide.

TENSION

Tension is not essential for this project.

YOU WILL NEED

◆ Scheepjes Metropolis, 75% wool, 25% nylon (219yd/200m per 50g ball): 1 ball in 031 Canberra (A)
◆ Scheepjes Merino Soft, 50% wool, 25% microfibre, 25% acrylic (115yd/105m per 50g ball): 1 ball in 607 Braque (B)
◆ 3.5mm (UK9:USE/4) crochet hook
◆ Cardboard for internal support
◆ Tapestry needle
◆ Plant pot approximately 3½in (9cm) in diameter

Note

The plant is worked in spirals using the amigurumi technique (see page 128). Make one side of the top of the heart then make a second and, without fastening off, crochet both together to form the heart.

Round 12: 10 dc, dc2tog, 18 dc, dc2tog, 10 dc (40 sts).

Rounds 13–14: Work 2 rounds straight (40 sts).

Round 15: 10 dc, dc2tog, 18 dc, dc2tog, 8 dc (38 sts).

Round 16: Work 1 round straight (38 sts).

Round 17: 10 dc, dc2tog, 17 dc, dc2tog, 7 dc (36 sts).

Round 18: Work 1 round straight (36 sts).

Round 19: 10 dc, dc2tog, 16 dc, dc2tog, 6 dc (34 sts).

Round 20: Work 1 round straight (34 sts).

Round 21: 10 dc, dc2tog, 15 dc, dc2tog, 5 dc (32 sts).

Round 22: 10 dc, dc2tog, 14 dc, dc2tog, 4 dc (30 sts).

Fasten off and leave a yarn tail to sew to the soil.

Leaf

Using 3.5mm hook and A, make a magic ring (see page 129).

Round 1: 1 ch, 6 dc into the centre of the ring.

Round 2: 2 dc into each st (12 sts).

Round 3: (1 dc, dc2inc) 6 times (18 sts).

Round 4: (8 dc, dc2inc) twice (20 sts).

Round 5: (9 dc, dc2inc) twice (22 sts).

Fasten off the first top.

Make a second, but do not fasten off.

Round 6: Work 22 sts around the first top and then 22 sts around the second, joining both together (44 sts).

Rounds 7–8: Work 2 rounds straight (44 sts).

Round 9: 10 dc, dc2tog, 20 dc, dc2tog, 10 dc (42 sts).

Rounds 10–11: Work 2 rounds straight (42 sts).

Soil

Using 3.5mm hook and B, make
a magic ring.

Round 1: 1 ch, 6 dc into the centre of
the ring.

Round 2: 2 dc into each st (12 sts).

Round 3: (1 dc, dc2inc) 6 times (18 sts).

Round 4: (2 dc, dc2inc) 6 times (24 sts).

Round 5: (3 dc, dc2inc) 6 times (30 sts).

Round 6: (4 dc, dc2inc) 6 times (36 sts).

Rounds 7–14: Work 8 rounds straight.

Round 15: (4 dc, dc2tog) 6 times (30 sts).

Round 16: (3 dc, dc2tog) 6 times (24 sts).

Round 17: (2 dc, dc2tog) 6 times (18 sts).
Stuff firmly with polyester stuffing.

Round 18: (1 dc, dc2tog) 6 times (12 sts).

Round 19: (Dc2tog) 6 times (6 sts).
Using a tapestry needle, weave this
yarn through the last dc sts of the
round and gather hole together.
Fasten off and weave in ends.

Making up

Flatten each leaf with the
palm of your hand. Place the
leaf on some thick cardboard
and draw around it with a
pencil to make an outline. Cut
out the cardboard shape just
a little inside the outline. Place
the cardboard inside the leaf.
Using the tails of yarn, sew
firmly to the soil and place
in the pot.

Sedum morganianum

Donkey's Tail

Overflowing with thick reams of grape-like succulents, this plant has a luxuriant look to it and is often found hanging in bathrooms. You could extend the luscious vines further by adding chain stitches to the pattern.

FINISHED SIZE

The longest strands are approximately 6in (15cm) long.

TENSION

Tension is not essential for this project.

YOU WILL NEED

- Scheepjes River Washed, 78% cotton, 22% acrylic (142yd/130m per 50g ball):
  1 ball in 962 Narmada (A)
- Scheepjes Merino Soft, 50% wool, 25% microfibre, 25% acrylic (115yd/105m per 50g ball):
  1 ball in 607 Braque (B)
- 3.5mm (UK9:USE/4) crochet hook
- Polyester stuffing
- Tapestry needle
- Plant pot approximately 2¾in (6cm) in diameter

Note

This plant's distinctive leaf structure is recreated using loop stitch (see page 131).

Small vine
(make 3)

Using 3.5mm hook and A, ch 11 sts.
Row 1: 1 dc in second ch from hook, dc to end, turn.
Row 2: 1 ch, work 1 loop in st at base of ch, and then in every dc to end, turn and work down the other side of the chain sts (20 loops).
Fasten off and leave a tail of yarn.

Medium vine
(make 3)

Using 3.5mm hook and A, ch 21 sts.
Row 1: 1 dc in second ch from hook, dc to end, turn.
Row 2: 1 ch, work 1 loop in st at base of ch, and then in every dc to end, turn and work down the other side of the chain sts (40 loops).
Fasten off and leave a tail of yarn.

Large vine
(make 2)

Using 3.5mm hook and A, ch 31 sts.
Row 1: 1 dc in second ch from hook, dc to end, turn.
Row 2: 1 ch, work 1 loop in st at base of ch, and then in every dc to end, turn and work down the other side of the chain sts (60 loops).
Fasten off and leave a tail of yarn.

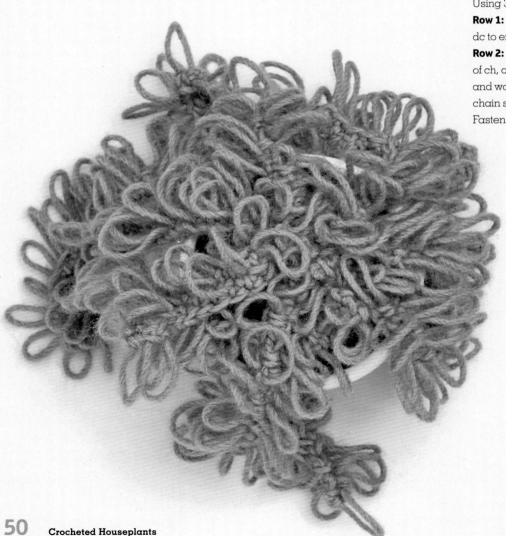

Soil

Using 3.5mm hook and B, make a magic ring (see page 129).

Round 1: 1 ch, 6 dc into the centre of the ring.

Round 2: 2 dc into each st (12 sts).

Round 3: (1 dc, dc2inc) 6 times (18 sts).

Round 4: (2 dc, dc2inc) 6 times (24 sts).

Rounds 5–12: Work 8 rounds straight.

Round 13: (2 dc, dc2tog) 6 times (18 sts). Stuff firmly with polyester stuffing.

Round 14: (1 dc, dc2tog) 6 times (12 sts).

Round 15: (Dc2tog) 6 times (6 sts). Using a tapestry needle, weave this yarn through the last dc sts of the round and gather hole together. Fasten off and weave in ends.

Making up

Using the tails of yarn, sew the end of the vines to the centre of the soil.

Curly Jade Plant

This is a very satisfying project to make. By increasing on every round in every row, you create a hyperbolic shape, which appears frequently in nature. This plant is made up of a number of undulating leaves. For extra realism, try using a variegated yarn.

FINISHED SIZE

The cactus is approximately 4¾in (12cm) in diameter.

TENSION

Tension is not essential for this project.

YOU WILL NEED

- Scheepjes Our Tribe, 30% polyamide, 70% wool, (459yd/420m per 100g ball): 1 ball in 977 A Spoonful of Yarn (A)
- Scheepjes Merino Soft, 50% wool, 25% microfibre, 25% acrylic (115yd/105m per 50g ball): 1 ball in 607 Braque (B)
- 3.5mm (UK9:USE/4) crochet hook
- Polyester stuffing
- Tapestry needle
- Plant pot approximately 4in (10cm) in diameter

Note

The leaves are worked in spirals using the amigurumi technique (see page 128). Place a marker at the beginning of each round so you know where you are in the pattern.

Leaves (make 6)

Using 3.5mm hook and A, make a magic ring (see page 129).

Round 1: 1 ch, 8 dc into the centre of the ring.

Round 2: 2 dc into each st (16 sts).

Round 3: 2 dc into each st (32 sts).

Round 4: 2 dc into each st (64 sts).

Round 5: 2 dc into each st (128 sts).

Round 6: 2 dc into each st (256 sts).

Round 7: 2 dc into each st (512 sts).

Fasten off and weave in ends.

Soil

Using 3.5mm hook and B, make a magic ring.

Round 1: 1 ch, 6 dc into the centre of the ring.

Round 2: 2 dc into each st (12 sts).

Round 3: (1 dc, dc2inc) 6 times (18 sts).

Round 4: (2 dc, dc2inc) 6 times (24 sts).

Round 5: (3 dc, dc2inc) 6 times (30 sts).

Round 6: (4 dc, dc2inc) 6 times (36 sts).

Round 7: (5 dc, dc2inc) 6 times (42 sts).

Round 8: (6 dc, dc2inc) 6 times (48 sts).

Rounds 9–16: Work 8 rounds straight.

Round 17: (6 dc, dc2tog) 6 times (42 sts).

Round 18: (5 dc, dc2tog) 6 times (36 sts).

Round 19: (4 dc, dc2tog) 6 times (30 sts).

Round 20: (3 dc, dc2tog) 6 times (24 sts).

Round 21: (2 dc, dc2tog) 6 times (18 sts).

Stuff firmly with polyester stuffing.

Round 22: (1 dc, dc2tog) 6 times (12 sts).

Round 23: (Dc2tog) 6 times (6 sts).

Using a tapestry needle, weave this yarn through the last dc sts of the round and gather hole together. Fasten off and weave in ends.

Making up

Arrange the ruffles so there are the maximum number of folds on display. Sew the very centre of the leaves firmly to the soil before placing in the pot.

Coleus

This glamorous plant features bright colours that look magnificent recreated in vibrant yarns. The real plant is not easy to keep in the house, so why not make a woolly one instead? I used a soft chunky yarn that replicates the textured leaves of the living version.

FINISHED SIZE

Each large leaf is approximately 6½in (16cm) long and 4in (10cm) wide.

TENSION

Tension is not essential for this project.

YOU WILL NEED

- West Yorkshire Spinners Retreat, 100% wool (153yd/140m per 100g ball): 1 ball in 692 Bliss (A), 738 Calm (B) and 452 Serene (C)
- Scheepjes Merino Soft, 50% wool, 25% microfibre, 25% acrylic (115yd/105m per 50g ball): 1 ball in 607 Braque (D)
- 3.5mm (UK9:USE/4) crochet hook
- 4mm (UK8:USG/6) crochet hook
- Tapestry needle
- Floristry wire
- Plant pot approximately 4¾in (12cm) in diameter

Note

This plant's distinctive pattern is recreated using spike stitch (see page 134).

Large leaf
(make 8)

Using 4mm hook and A, ch 12 sts.

Round 1: 1 dc in 2nd ch, 1 htr, 1 tr, tr2inc, dtr2inc, 1dtr, dtr2inc, tr2inc, 1 tr, 1 htr, 1 dc in last ch, (now turn and work down the other side of the foundation ch), 4 ch, 1 dc in 3rd ch from hook 1 ch, 1 dc in first ch of foundation ch, 1 htr, 1 tr, tr2inc, dtr2inc, 1dtr, dtr2inc, tr2inc, 1 tr, 1 htr, 1 dc, 1 sl st into turning ch, 1 ch.

Round 2: Working into sts of first row, 14 dc, (3 dc, 2 ch, 3 dc) in 3 ch at the tip of the leaf, 14 dc, 1 ch, sl st into last ch of previous round.
Fasten off yarn A.

Round 3: Change to yarn B, 3 dc in first st of previous round, 2 dc, 1 spike, 3 dc, 1 spike, 2 dc, 1 spike, 3 dc, 1 spike, 4 dc, (1 dc, 2 ch, 1 dc) into ch sp at the tip of the leaf, 4 dc, 1 spike, 3 dc, 1 spike, 2 dc, 1 spike, 3 dc, 1 spike, 2 dc, 2 dc in last ch of previous round.

Round 4: Dc2inc in first st, dc2inc, 1 tr, 6 tr2inc, 2 htr, htr2inc, 3 htr, 6 dc, 3 ch, 6 dc, 3 htr, htr2inc, 2 htr, 6 tr2inc, 1 tr, 2 dc2inc.
Fasten off yarn B.

Round 5: Change to yarn C, 10 dc, 1 spike, 3 dc, 1 spike, 3 htr, 1 spike, 2 htr, 1 spike, 1 htr, 1 spike, 1 htr, 1 spike, 5 tr, 6 tr in 3 ch sp at tip of leaf, 5 tr, 1 spike, 1 htr, 1 spike, 1 htr, 1 spike, 2 htr, 1 spike, 3 htr, 1 spike, 3 dc, 1 spike, 10 dc, sl st into first dc.
Fasten off and weave in all ends.

Small leaf
(make 2)

Using 4mm hook and A, ch 8 sts.

Round 1: 1 dc in 2nd ch, 1 htr, 1 tr, 2 htr, 1 dc in last ch, (now turn and work down the other side of the foundation ch), 2 ch, 1 dc in first ch of foundation ch, 2 htr, 1 tr, 1 htr, 1 dc, sl st into turning ch, 1 ch.
Fasten off yarn A.

Round 2: Change to yarn B, working into sts of first row, dc2inc, 1 dc, 3 htr, tr2inc, 2 tr2inc in ch sp at tip of leaf, tr2inc, 3 htr, 1 dc, dc2inc, sl st into turn ch.
Fasten off yarn B.

Round 3: Change to yarn C, 2 dc2inc, 4 dc, 2 dc2inc, 2 dc, 2 ch, 2 dc, 2 dc2inc, 4 dc, 2 dc2inc.
Fasten off and weave in all ends.

Soil

Using 3.5mm hook and D, make a magic ring (see page 129).

Round 1: 1 ch, 6 dc into the centre of the ring.

Round 2: 2 dc into each st (12 sts).

Round 3: (1 dc, dc2inc) 6 times (18 sts).

Round 4: (2 dc, dc2inc) 6 times (24 sts).

Round 5: (3 dc, dc2inc) 6 times (30 sts).

Round 6: (4 dc, dc2inc) 6 times (36 sts).

Round 7: (5 dc, dc2inc) 6 times (42 sts).

Round 8: (6 dc, dc2inc) 6 times (48 sts).

Rounds 9–16: Work 8 rounds straight.

Round 17: (6 dc, dc2tog) 6 times (42 sts).

Round 18: (5 dc, dc2tog) 6 times (36 sts).

Round 19: (4 dc, dc2tog) 6 times (30 sts).

Round 20: (3 dc, dc2tog) 6 times (24 sts).

Round 21: (2 dc, dc2tog) 6 times (18 sts).

Stuff firmly with polyester stuffing.

Round 22: (1 dc, dc2tog) 6 times (12 sts).

Round 23: (Dc2tog) 6 times (6 sts).

Using a tapestry needle, weave this yarn through the last dc sts of the round and gather hole together. Fasten off and weave in ends.

Making up

Weave a strand of floristry wire through the centre of the leaves on the wrong side. Arrange two large leaves to be opposite each other and sew to the soil. Place another two large leaves at right angles, and sew on top. Repeat so all eight large leaves have been placed.

Poke the end of the floristry wire on each strand through the soil and fold over the wire to secure. Sew the base of the leaf securely to the top of the soil. Finally, place the two small leaves in the centre and sew them securely in place. Manipulate the wire to create a natural plant shape.

Agave americana

Century Plant

One of the giants of the plant world, growing around
6–9ft high (2–3m), this gorgeous plant is graphic and striking.
In its (much smaller) woolly form, its spikes are
achieved using small picot stitches.

FINISHED SIZE

The plant is approximately
8in (20cm) in diameter.

TENSION

Tension is not essential for this project.

YOU WILL NEED

- Scheepjes Metropolis, 75% wool,
  25% nylon (219yd/200m per 50g ball):
  1 ball in 031 Canberra (A),
  026 Depok (B) and 033 Atlanta (C)
- Scheepjes Merino Soft, 50% wool,
  25% microfibre, 25% acrylic
  (115yd/105m per 50g ball):
  1 ball in 607 Braque (D)
- 3mm (UK11:US–) crochet hook
- 3.5mm (UK9:USE/4) crochet hook
- Polyester stuffing
- Tapestry needle
- Floristry wire
- Plant pot approximately
  4in (10cm) in diameter

Note

*The leaves are worked in
rows, working on both
sides of the foundation
chain stitches.*

Large leaf (make 7)

Using 3mm hook and A, ch 24 sts around a wire (see page 133).

Row 1: 1 dc in 2nd ch from hook, 1 dc in each st to end, turn (23 sts). Fasten off yarn A.

Row 2 WS: Change to yarn B, sl st in first dc, 1 ch, 1 sl st in base of ch, 3 sl st, 5 dc, 4 htr, 3 tr, 4 htr, 2 dc, dc2inc, 1 ch, (now turn and work down the other side of the foundation ch), dc2inc, 2 dc, 4 htr, 3 tr, 4 htr, 5 dc, 4 sl st, turn (49 sts). Fasten off yarn B.

Row 3 RS: Change to yarn C, attach yarn with sl st, 1 ch, 1 dc at base of ch, 3 dc, 2 htr, 12 tr, 1 htr, 5 dc, (1 dtr, 3 ch, 1 sl st), in turning ch, (now turn and work down the other side of the leaf), 5 dc, 1 htr, 12 tr, 2 htr, 4 dc, turn (50 sts).

Row 4 WS: 1 ch, 1 sl st at base of ch, * 2 sl st, (1 sl st, 2 ch, 1 sl st) into next st; rep from * 6 times, 2 sl st, 1 sl st in ch sp, (1 sl st, 2 ch, 1 sl st) in top of dtr at the point of the leaf, 1 sl st in side of dtr, ** 2 sl st, (1 sl st, 2 ch, 1 sl st) into next st; rep from * 6 times, 3 sl st. Fasten off and leave a tail of yarn.

Small leaf (make 3)

A central wire is not needed for this leaf.

Using 3mm hook and A, ch 6 sts.

Row 1: 1 dc in 2nd ch from hook, 1 dc in each st to end, turn (5 sts). Fasten off yarn A.

Row 2 WS: Change to yarn B, 1 ch, 1 dc in base of ch, 4 dc, 2 ch, (now turn and work down the other side of the foundation ch), 5 dc (12 sts). Fasten off yarn B.

Row 3 RS: Change to yarn C, attach yarn with sl st, 1 ch, 2 dc at base of ch, 4 dc, 1 dc in ch sp, 2 ch, sl st in same ch sp, (now turn and work down the other side of the leaf) 4 dc, dc2inc. Fasten off and leave a tail of yarn.

Soil

Using 3.5mm hook and D, make a magic ring (see page 129).

Round 1: 1 ch, 6 dc into the centre of the ring.

Round 2: 2 dc into each st (12 sts).

Round 3: (1 dc, dc2inc) 6 times (18 sts).

Round 4: (2 dc, dc2inc) 6 times (24 sts).

Round 5: (3 dc, dc2inc) 6 times (30 sts).

Round 6: (4 dc, dc2inc) 6 times (36 sts).

Round 7: (5 dc, dc2inc) 6 times (42 sts).

Round 8: (6 dc, dc2inc) 6 times (48 sts).

Rounds 9–16: Work 8 rounds straight.

Round 17: (6 dc, dc2tog) 6 times (42 sts).

Round 18: (5 dc, dc2tog) 6 times (36 sts).

Round 19: (4 dc, dc2tog) 6 times (30 sts).

Round 20: (3 dc, dc2tog) 6 times (24 sts).

Round 21: (2 dc, dc2tog) 6 times (18 sts). Stuff firmly with polyester stuffing.

Round 22: (1 dc, dc2tog) 6 times (12 sts).

Round 23: (Dc2tog) 6 times (6 sts).

Using a tapestry needle, weave this yarn through the last dc sts of the round and gather hole together. Fasten off and weave in ends.

Making up

Arrange the seven large leaves to form a star. Poke the end of the floristry wire on each strand through the soil and fold over the wire to secure. Sew the base of the leaf securely to the top of the soil. Equally space the three small leaves to form a trefoil, sew these together to ensure their spacing is even, then sew on top of your large leaves on the crocheted soil. Manipulate the wire to create a natural plant shape.

Yucca

The yucca is making a comeback, due to its angular good looks and exotic feel. This dramatic plant has long, sword-like, yellow-green arching leaves that grow in a rosette from the top of a bare trunk.

FINISHED SIZE

The plant in its pot is approximately 12in (30cm) tall from the base of the trunk to the top of the leaves.

YOU WILL NEED

- Scheepjes Metropolis, 75% wool, 25% nylon (219yd/200m per 50g ball): 1 ball in 032 Abu Dhabi (A) and 031 Canberra (B)
- Sirdar Haworth Tweed DK, 50% nylon, 50% wool (180yd/165m per 50g ball): 1 ball in 910 Harewood Chestnut (C)
- Scheepjes Merino Soft, 50% wool, 25% microfibre, 25% acrylic (115yd/105m per 50g ball): 1 ball in 607 Braque (D)
- 3mm (UK11:US–) crochet hook
- 3.5mm (UK9:USE/4) crochet hook
- Polyester stuffing
- Tapestry needle
- Floristry wire
- Cardboard tube such as toilet roll
- Plant pot approximately 4¾in (12cm) in diameter

TENSION

Tension is not essential for this project.

Note

The trunk is made by encasing the inner cardboard tube of a toilet roll. The plant leaves are worked in rows. Create strength in the leaf by working around a wire on row 2 (see page 133). Work one side of the leaf, then the other side, and then complete the leaf by working a final row of dc in yarn A or B.

Trunk

Using 3.5mm hook and C, make a
magic ring (see page 129).
Round 1: 1 ch, 7 dc into the centre
of the ring.
Round 2: 2 dc into each st (14 sts).
Round 3: (1 dc, dc2inc) 7 times (21 sts).
Round 4: 1 dc in each st (21 sts).
Rounds 5–22: Work 18 rounds straight
tbl (21 sts).

Very large leaf
(make 4)

Make 2 using A and 2 using B.
Row 1: Using 3mm hook, ch 45 sts.
Hold your floristry wire above your ch
sts; you will work around the wire to
encase it in the crochet.
Row 2: Insert your hook into the 2nd st
from the hook, yarn over the hook, pull
through the stitch, put your hook over
the wire and the stitches and wrap the
yarn over the hook and pull through

both loops on the hook, encasing the
wire. Rep to the end of the ch stitches,
pm, turn (44 sts).
Pull the wire so that it is at
the beginning of the row.
Row 3 WS: Ch 1, 40 dc,
4 sl st, 1 ch, (now work down the other
side of the leaf into the other side of the
ch sts), 4 sl st, 40 dc, turn (89 sts).
Row 4 RS: Ch 1, 40 dc, 4 sl st, (1 sl st, 2 ch,
1 sl st) in ch sp, 4 sl st, 40 dc.
Fasten off and leave a tail of yarn.

Large leaf
(make 4)

Row 1: Using 3mm hook and A, ch 37 sts.
Hold your floristry wire above your ch
sts; you will work around the wire to
encase it in the crochet.
Row 2: Insert your hook into the 2nd st
from the hook, yarn over the hook, pull
through the stitch, put your hook over
the wire and the stitches and wrap the
yarn over the hook and pull through
both loops on the hook, encasing the
wire. Rep to the end of the ch stitches,
pm, turn (36 sts).
Pull the wire so that it is at the beginning
of the row.
Row 3 WS: Ch 1, 32 dc, 4 sl st, 1 ch, (now
work down the other side of the leaf into
the other side of the ch sts), 4 sl st, 32 dc,
turn (73 sts).
Fasten off yarn A and leave a long tail
of yarn.
Row 4 RS: Ch 1, 32 dc, 4 sl st, (1 sl st,
2 ch, 1 sl st) in ch sp, 4 sl st, 32 dc.
Fasten off and leave a tail of yarn.

Medium leaf
(make 5)

Make 2 using A and 3 using B.
Row 1: Using 3mm hook, ch 31 sts.
Hold your floristry wire above your ch
sts; you will work around the wire to
encase it in the crochet.
Row 2: Insert your hook into the 2nd st
from the hook, yarn over the hook, pull
through the stitch, put your hook over
the wire and the stitches and wrap the
yarn over the hook and pull through
both loops on the hook, encasing the
wire. Rep to the end of the ch stitches,
pm, turn (30 sts).
Pull the wire so that
it is at the beginning
of the row.
Row 3 WS: Ch 1, 26 dc, 4 sl
st, 1 ch, (now
work down the
other side of the
leaf into the other side of
the ch sts), 4 sl st, 26 dc, turn (61 sts).
Row 4 RS: Ch 1, 26 dc, 4 sl st, (1 sl st,
2 ch, 1 sl st) in ch sp, 4 sl st, 26 dc.
Fasten off and leave a tail of yarn.

Small leaf
(make 2)

Row 1: Using 3mm hook and A, ch
21 sts.
Hold your floristry wire above your ch
sts; you will work around the wire to
encase it in the crochet.
Row 2: Insert your hook into the 2nd st
from the hook, yarn over the hook, pull
through the stitch, put your hook over
the wire and the stitches and wrap the
yarn over the hook and pull through
both loops on the hook, encasing the
wire. Rep to the end of the ch stitches,
pm, turn (20 sts).

Pull the wire so that it is at the beginning of the row.

Row 3 WS: Ch 1, 16 dc, 4 sl st, 1 ch, (now work down the other side of the leaf into the other side of the ch sts), 4 sl st, 16 dc, turn (41 sts).

Fasten off yarn A and leave a long tail of yarn.

Row 4 RS: Ch 1, 16 dc, 4 sl st, (1 sl st, 2 ch, 1 sl st) in ch sp, 4 sl st, 16 dc. Fasten off and leave a tail of yarn.

Baby leaves (make 3)

Row 1: Using 3mm hook and A, ch 11 sts. Hold your floristry wire above your ch sts; you will work around the wire to encase it in the crochet.

Row 2: Insert your hook into the 2nd st from the hook, yarn over the hook, pull through the stitch, put your hook over the wire and the stitches and wrap the yarn over the hook and pull through both loops on the hook, encasing the wire. Rep to the end of the ch stitches, pm, turn (10 sts).

Pull the wire so that it is at the beginning of the row, then cut off the wire to fit the chain stitches. Weave in all ends.

Row 3 WS: Ch 1, 8 dc, 2 sl st, 1 ch, (now work down the other side of the leaf into the other side of the ch sts), 2 sl st, 8 dc, turn (21 sts).

Fasten off yarn A and leave a long tail of yarn.

Soil

Using 3.5mm hook and D, make a magic ring (see page 129).

Round 1: 1 ch, 6 dc into the centre of the ring.

Round 2: 2 dc into each st (12 sts).

Round 3: (1 dc, dc2inc) 6 times (18 sts).

Round 4: (2 dc, dc2inc) 6 times (24 sts).

Round 5: (3 dc, dc2inc) 6 times (30 sts).

Round 6: (4 dc, dc2inc) 6 times (36 sts).

Round 7: (5 dc, dc2inc) 6 times (42 sts).

Round 8: (6 dc, dc2inc) 6 times (48 sts).

Round 9: (7 dc, dc2inc) 6 times (54 sts).

Round 10: (8 dc, dc2inc) 6 times (60 sts).

Rounds 11–18: Work 8 rounds straight.

Round 19: (8 dc, dc2tog) 6 times (54 sts).

Round 20: (7 dc, dc2tog) 6 times (48 sts).

Round 21: (6 dc, dc2tog) 6 times (42 sts).

Round 22: (5 dc, dc2tog) 6 times (36 sts).

Round 23: (4 dc, dc2tog) 6 times (30 sts).

Round 24: (3 dc, dc2tog) 6 times (24 sts).

Round 25: (2 dc, dc2tog) 6 times (18 sts).

Stuff firmly with polyester stuffing.

Round 26: (1 dc, dc2tog) 6 times (12 sts).

Round 27: (Dc2tog) 6 times (6 sts).

Using a tapestry needle, weave this yarn through the last dc sts of the round and gather hole together. Fasten off and weave in ends.

Making up

Cover a cardboard tube such as the inside of a toilet roll with the crochet for the trunk. Stuff the trunk firmly with stuffing. Place in the centre of the soil and, using a tail of yarn, sew firmly to the soil. Poke the wire of each very large, large, medium and small leaf into the top of the trunk and use the long tails of yarn to sew the base of the leaf securely to the top of the trunk. Attach the baby leaves in a clump to the side of the trunk. Twist the leaves slightly to create a natural plant shape.

Inch Plant

This plant earned its Latin name due to its zebra-like stripes and can be found in many different colours. Whether in living or crocheted form, it looks beautiful when arranged to trail off a shelf or a mantlepiece.

FINISHED SIZE

The leaves are approximately 10in (25cm) long and 1¾in (4cm) wide.

TENSION

Tension is not essential for this project.

YOU WILL NEED

- Scheepjes Catona, 100% cotton (136yd/125m per 50g ball):
  1 ball in 394 Shadow Purple (A) and 226 Light Orchid (B)
- Scheepjes Merino Soft, 50% wool, 25% microfibre, 25% acrylic (115yd/105m per 50g ball):
  1 ball in 607 Braque (C)
- 3mm (UK11:US–) crochet hook
- 3.5mm (UK9:USE/4) crochet hook
- Polyester stuffing
- Tapestry needle
- Floristry wire
- Plant pot approximately 4in (10cm) in diameter

Note

The plant leaves are worked in rows. Work one side of the leaf, then the other side and then finish with a row of dc in yarn B or A. Create strength in the stem by working around a wire on row 2 (see page 133).

Striped leaf
(make 43)

Using 3mm hook and A, ch 6 sts.
Row 1: 1 dc in 2nd ch from hook, 1 dc in each st to end, turn (5 sts).
Row 2 RS: Change to yarn B, 1 ch, 1 dc in base of ch, 4 dc, 2 ch, (now turn and work down the other side of the foundation ch), 5 dc (12 sts).
Fasten off yarn B.
Row 3 RS: Change to yarn A, attach yarn with sl st, 1 ch, 2 dc at base of ch, 4 dc, 1 dc in ch sp, 2 ch, sl st in same ch sp, (now turn and work down the other side of the leaf), 4 dc, dc2inc.
Fasten off and leave a tail of yarn.

Plain leaf
(make 7)

Using 3mm hook and A, ch 6 sts.
Row 1: 1 dc in 2nd ch from hook, 1 dc in each st to end, turn (5 sts).
Row 2 RS: 1 ch, 1 dc in base of ch, 4 dc, 2 ch, (now turn and work down the other side of the foundation ch), 5 dc (12 sts).
Fasten off and leave a tail of yarn.

Large stem
(make 4)

Row 1: Using 3mm hook and A, ch 41 sts.
Hold your floristry wire above your ch sts; you will work around the wire to encase it in the crochet.
Row 2: Insert your hook into the 2nd st from the hook, yarn over the hook, pull through the stitch, put your hook over the wire and the stitches and wrap the yarn over the hook and pull through both loops on the hook, encasing the wire. Rep to the end of the ch stitches, pm, turn (40 sts).
Pull the wire so that it is at the beginning of the row.
Fasten off and leave a tail of yarn.

Small stem
(make 3)

Row 1: Using 3mm hook and A, ch 31 sts.
Hold your floristry wire above your ch sts; you will work around the wire to encase it in the crochet.

Row 2: Insert your hook into the 2nd st from the hook, yarn over the hook, pull through the stitch, put your hook over the wire and the stitches and wrap the yarn over the hook and pull through both loops on the hook, encasing the wire. Rep to the end of the ch stitches, pm, turn (30 sts).
Pull the wire so that it is at the beginning of the row.
Fasten off and leave a tail of yarn.

Soil

Using 3.5mm hook and C, make a magic ring (see page 129).

Round 1: 1 ch, 6 dc into the centre of the ring.
Round 2: 2 dc into each st (12 sts).
Round 3: (1 dc, dc2inc) 6 times (18 sts).
Round 4: (2 dc, dc2inc) 6 times (24 sts).
Round 5: (3 dc, dc2inc) 6 times (30 sts).
Round 6: (4 dc, dc2inc) 6 times (36 sts).
Round 7: (5 dc, dc2inc) 6 times (42 sts).
Round 8: (6 dc, dc2inc) 6 times (48 sts).

Rounds 9–16: Work 8 rounds straight.
Round 17: (6 dc, dc2tog) 6 times (42 sts).
Round 18: (5 dc, dc2tog) 6 times (36 sts).
Round 19: (4 dc, dc2tog) 6 times (30 sts).
Round 20: (3 dc, dc2tog) 6 times (24 sts).
Round 21: (2 dc, dc2tog) 6 times (18 sts).
Stuff firmly with polyester stuffing.
Round 22: (1 dc, dc2tog) 6 times (12 sts).
Round 23: (Dc2tog) 6 times (6 sts).
Using a tapestry needle, weave this yarn through the last dc sts of the round and gather hole together.
Fasten off and weave in ends.

Making up

Weave in the stray ends of yarn B on each leaf. Poke the wire of each leaf into the soil and then use the long tails of yarn A to sew the stems securely to the top of the soil. Sew a plain leaf at the end of each stem and then sew striped leaves evenly up the stem approximately six stitches apart, five on each small stem and seven on each large stem. Curl the stems slightly to create a natural plant shape.

Chinese Money Plant

This distinctive houseplant from southern China is very popular due to its UFO-like circular leaves. It is also sometimes known as a 'pancake plant' because of the flat, round leaves. A woolly version will make an attractive addition to your collection.

FINISHED SIZE

Plant is approximately 3½in (9cm) tall.

YOU WILL NEED

- Stylecraft Special DK, 100% acrylic (323yd/295m per 100g ball): Small amounts in 1852 Apple Green (A) and 1004 Dark Brown (B)
- 3.5mm (UK9:USE/4) crochet hook
- Polyester stuffing
- Tapestry needle
- Floristry wire
- Plant pot approximately 4in (10cm) in diameter

TENSION

Tension is not essential for this project.

Note

The project is worked in spirals using the amigurumi technique (see page 128). Place a marker at the beginning of each round so you know where you are in the pattern.

Large leaf
(make 3)

Using 3.5mm hook and A, make a magic ring (see page 129).

Round 1: 1 ch, 8 dc into the centre of the ring.

Round 2: 2 dc into each st (16 sts).

Round 3: Work 1 round straight.

Round 4: (1 dc, dc2inc) 8 times (24 sts).

Round 5: Work 1 round straight.

Round 6: (2 dc, dc2inc) 8 times (32 sts).

Round 7: Work 1 round straight.

Round 8: Work 1 round straight blo.

Round 9: (2 dc, dc2tog) 8 times (24 sts).

Round 10: Work 1 round straight.

Round 11: (1 dc, dc2tog) 8 times (16 sts).

Round 12: Work 1 round straight.

Round 13: (Dc2tog) 8 times (8 sts).

Fasten off and leave a long yarn tail.

Small leaf
(make 4)

Using 3.5mm hook and A, make a magic ring.

Round 1: 1 ch, 8 dc into the centre of the ring.

Round 2: 2 dc into each st (16 sts).

Round 3: Work 1 round straight.

Round 4: (1 dc, dc2inc) 8 times (24 sts).

Round 5: Work 1 round straight.

Round 6: Work 1 round straight blo.

Round 7: (1 dc, dc2tog) 8 times (16 sts).

Round 8: Work 1 round straight.

Round 9: (Dc2tog) 8 times (8 sts).

Fasten off and leave a long yarn tail.

Large stalk
(make 1)

Row 1: Using 3.5mm hook and A, ch 17 sts.

Hold your floristry wire above your ch sts; you will work around the wire to encase it in the crochet (see page 133).

Row 2: Insert your hook into the 2nd st from the hook, yarn over the hook, pull through the stitch, put your hook over the wire and the stitches and wrap the yarn over the hook and pull through both loops on the hook, encasing the wire. Rep to the end of the ch stitches. (16 sts).

Pull the wire so that it is at the beginning of the row.

Fasten off and leave a long tail.

Medium stalk
(make 2)

Row 1: Using 3.5mm hook and A, ch 15 sts.

Hold your floristry wire above your ch sts; you will work around the wire to encase it in the crochet.

Row 2: Insert your hook into the 2nd st from the hook, yarn over the hook, pull through the stitch, put your hook over the wire and the stitches and wrap the yarn over the hook and pull through both loops on the hook, encasing the wire. Rep to the end of the ch stitches. (14 sts).

Pull the wire so that it is at the beginning of the row.

Fasten off and leave a long tail.

Round 3: (1 dc, dc2inc) 6 times (18 sts).
Round 4: (2 dc, dc2inc) 6 times (24 sts).
Round 5: (3 dc, dc2inc) 6 times (30 sts).
Round 6: (4 dc, dc2inc) 6 times (36 sts).
Round 7: (5 dc, dc2inc) 6 times (42 sts).
Round 8: (6 dc, dc2inc) 6 times (48 sts).
Rounds 9–16: Work 8 rounds straight.
Round 17: (6 dc, dc2tog) 6 times (42 sts).
Round 18: (5 dc, dc2tog) 6 times (36 sts).
Round 19: (4 dc, dc2tog) 6 times (30 sts).
Round 20: (3 dc, dc2tog) 6 times (24 sts).
Round 21: (2 dc, dc2tog) 6 times (18 sts).
Stuff firmly with polyester stuffing.
Round 22: (1 dc, dc2tog) 6 times (12 sts).
Round 23: (Dc2tog) 6 times (6 sts).
Using a tapestry needle, weave this
yarn through the last dc sts of the
round and gather hole together.
Fasten off and weave in ends.

Making up

Flatten the leaf using the palm
of your hand. Use the tail of
yarn to make some small
stitches to sew both sides of
the leaf together. Then sew
one large leaf to the top of the
large stalk, slightly off centre.
Push the floristry wire through
the centre of the soil and bend
the wire over. At the base of
the crochet stalk, use the tail
of yarn to sew the stalk firmly
to the top of the soil. Repeat,
sewing two large leaves to
medium stalks and the small
leaves to small stalks. Make
sure each stalk is sewn firmly
to the soil at its base.

Small stalk (make 4)

Row 1: Using 3.5mm hook and A,
ch 11 sts.
Hold your floristry wire above your ch
sts; you will work around the wire to
encase it in the crochet.
Row 2: Insert your hook into the 2nd st
from the hook, yarn over the hook, pull
through the stitch, put your hook over
the wire and the stitches and wrap the
yarn over the hook and pull through
both loops on the hook, encasing the
wire. Rep to the end of the ch stitches.
(10 sts).
Pull the wire so that it is at the
beginning of the row.
Fasten off and leave a long tail.

Soil

Using 3.5mm hook and B, make
a magic ring.
Round 1: 1 ch, 6 dc into the centre
of the ring.
Round 2: 2 dc into each st (12 sts).

Rebutia krainziana

Crown Cactus

This neat little cactus produces brightly coloured flowers, which makes it very popular as a houseplant. Choose an equally vibrant yarn to do justice to your crocheted version.

FINISHED SIZE

The cactus is approximately 2¾in (7cm) tall and wide.

YOU WILL NEED

- Scheepjes Metropolis, 75% wool, 25% nylon (219yd/200m per 50g ball): 1 ball in 031 Canberra (A)
- Sirdar Happy Cotton, 100% cotton (47yd/43m per 20g ball): Small amount of 788 Quack (B) and 753 Freckle (C)
- Scheepjes Merino Soft, 50% wool, 25% microfibre, 25% acrylic (115yd/105m per 50g ball): 1 ball in 607 Braque (D)
- 3.5mm (UK9:USE/4) crochet hook
- Polyester stuffing
- Tapestry needle
- The toe of a clean dark stocking or sock

- Plant pot approximately 3in (7.5cm) in diameter

TENSION

Tension is not essential for this project.

Note

The cactus is worked in spirals using the amigurumi technique (see page 128). Puff stitches are placed in the spaces between the stitches of the previous round. Place a marker at the beginning of each round so you know where you are in the pattern.

Special abbreviations

Puff stitch: *Yrh, insert into st, yrh and draw loop through st, drawing loop up to the height of the sts in the row; rep from * twice into the same stitch, 7 loops on the hook, yrh and draw loop through all loops on hook. Puff completed.

Puff2inc: Work 2 puff sts in one st sp.

Puff2tog: *Yrh, insert into st, yrh and draw loop through st, drawing loop up to the height of the sts in the row; rep from * twice into the same stitch, 7 loops on the hook, rep into next st sp, yrh and draw loop through all 14 loops on hook. Puff dec completed.

Cactus

Using 3.5mm hook and A, make a magic ring (see page 129).

Round 1: 1 ch, 6 dc into the centre of the ring.

Round 2: 2 dc into each st (12 sts).

Round 3: 1 puff in each sp (12 puffs).

Round 4: (1 puff in sp before the next st, puff2inc in next sp) 6 times (18 puffs).

Round 5: 1 puff in each sp (18 puffs).

Round 6: (2 puff, puff2inc in next sp) 6 times (24 puffs).

Rounds 7–10: 1 puff in each sp (24 puffs).

Round 11: (2 puff, puff2tog) 6 times (18 puffs).

Round 12: 1 puff in each sp (18 puffs).

Round 13: (Dc2tog) 9 times (9 sts). Fasten off and leave a yarn tail.

Spiky flower (make 1)

Using 3.5mm hook and B, make a magic ring.

Round 1: 1 ch, 9 dc into the centre of the ring, join with a sl st.

Round 2: Change to yarn C, (ch 6, miss 1 ch, 1 sl st along the rest of ch sts, sl st in same st), * sl st in next st, 6 ch, miss 1 ch, 1 sl st along the rest of ch sts, sl st in same st; rep from * 7 times. Fasten off, weave in yarn C and leave a yarn tail of B.

Soil

Using 3.5mm hook and D, make a magic ring.

Round 1: 1 ch, 6 dc into the centre of the ring.

Round 2: 2 dc into each st (12 sts).

Round 3: (1 dc, dc2inc) 6 times (18 sts).

Round 4: (2 dc, dc2inc) 6 times (24 sts).

Rounds 5–12: Work 8 rounds straight.

Round 13: (2 dc, dc2tog) 6 times (18 sts). Stuff firmly with polyester stuffing.

Round 14: (1 dc, dc2tog) 6 times (12 sts).

Round 15: (Dc2tog) 6 times (6 sts). Using a tapestry needle, weave this yarn through the last dc sts of the round and gather hole together. Fasten off and weave in ends.

Making up

Cut a sock or stocking approximately 2in (5cm) from the toe. Insert into the cactus to create a dark background to the puff stitches. Using the polyester stuffing, firmly stuff the cactus. Using the long tail of yarn, sew some small stitches along the last round of crochet and slightly pull them to gather the end together. Sew the flower firmly to the side of the cactus. Sew firmly to the top of the soil.

Swiss Cheese Plant

The Swiss cheese plant is the king of houseplants. They can grow to enormous sizes and the real version, as well as the crochet alternative, need staking to remain upright. This plant is distinguished by its heart-shaped glossy green foliage; the larger leaves have holes that resemble Swiss cheese.

FINISHED SIZE

The plant in its pot is approximately 12in (30cm) tall from the base of the stem to the top of the leaves.

TENSION

Tension is not essential for this project.

YOU WILL NEED

- Stylecraft Special DK, 100% acrylic (323yd/295m per 100g ball): 1 ball in 1009 Bottle (A) and 1004 Dark Brown (B)
- 4mm (UK8:USG/6) crochet hook
- 3.5mm (UK9:USE/4) crochet hook
- Polyester stuffing
- Tapestry needle
- 0.35mm floristry wire
- 1.2mm garden wire
- Plant stakes
- Plant pot approximately 4¾in (12cm) in diameter

Note

The stems are made by encasing plant stakes and wire with crochet. Create strength in the leaf by weaving floristry wire on the underside. It is useful to use a row counter for this project or a notebook to keep track of where you are in the pattern.

Small leaf
(make 2)

Using 4mm hook and A, ch 2 sts.
Row 1 RS: 3 dc in 2nd ch from hook, turn (3 sts).
Row 2 WS: 1 ch, 1 dc, (1 dc, 1 ch, 1 dc), 1 dc, turn (4 sts).
Row 3 RS: 1 ch, 2 dc, (1 dc, 1 ch, 1 dc) in next ch sp, 2 dc, turn (6 sts).
Row 4 WS: 1 ch, 3 dc, (1 dc, 1 ch, 1 dc) in next ch sp, 3 dc, turn (8 sts).
Row 5 RS: 1 ch, 4 dc, (1 dc, 1 ch, 1 dc) in next ch sp, 4 dc, turn (10 sts).
Row 6 WS: 1 ch, 5 dc, (1 dc, 1 ch, 1 dc) in next ch sp, 5 dc, turn (12 sts).
Row 7 RS: 1 ch, 6 dc, (1 dc, 1 ch, 1 dc) in next ch sp, 6 dc, turn (14 sts).
Row 8 WS: 1 ch, 7 dc, (1 dc, 1 ch, 1 dc) in next ch sp, 7 dc, turn (16 sts).
Row 9 RS: 1 ch, 8 dc, (1 dc, 1 ch, 1 dc) in next ch sp, 8 dc, turn (18 sts).
Row 10 WS: 1 ch, 9 dc, (1 dc, 1 ch, 1 dc) in next ch sp, 9 dc, turn (20 sts).
Row 11 RS: 1 ch, 10 dc, (1 dc, 1 ch, 1 dc) in next ch sp, 10 dc, turn (22 sts).
Row 12 WS: 1 ch, 11 dc, (1 dc, 1 ch, 1 dc) in next ch sp, 11 dc, turn (24 sts).
Row 13 RS: 1 ch, 12 dc, (1 dc, 1 ch, 1 dc) in next ch sp, 12 dc, turn (26 sts).
Row 14 WS: 1 ch, 13 dc, (1 dc, 1 ch, 1 dc) in next ch sp, 13 dc, turn (28 sts).
Row 15 RS: 1 ch, 14 dc, (1 dc, 1 ch, 1 dc) in next ch sp, 14 dc, turn (30 sts).
Row 16 WS: 1 ch, miss st at base of ch, 14 dc, (1 dc, 1 ch, 1 dc) in next ch sp, 13 dc, miss 1 st, 1 dc, turn (30 sts).
Row 17 RS: 1 ch, 15 dc, (1 dc, 1 ch, 1 dc) in next ch sp, 15 dc, turn (32 sts).
Row 18 WS: 1 ch, miss st at base of ch, 15 dc, (1 dc, 1 ch, 1 dc) in next ch sp, 14 dc, miss 1 st, 1 dc, turn (32 sts).
Row 19 RS: 1 ch, 16 dc, (1 dc, 1 ch, 1 dc) in next ch sp, 16 dc, turn (34 sts).
Row 20 WS: 1 ch, miss st at base of ch, 16 dc, (1 dc, 1 ch, 1 dc) in next ch sp, 15 dc, miss 1 st, 1 dc, turn (34 sts).
Rows 21–22: Rep row 20, twice (34 sts). This will create a straight edge.

You will now work the top of each side of the heart shape separately.

Right side of the leaf
Row 23 RS: 1 ch, 16 dc, turn (16 sts).
Row 24 WS: 1 ch, 16 dc, turn (16 sts).
Row 25 RS: 1 ch, dc2inc in st at base of ch, 13 dc, miss 1 st, 1 dc, turn (16 sts).
Row 26 WS: 1 ch, miss 1 st, 12 dc, miss 2 sts, 1 dc, turn (13 sts).
Row 27 RS: 1 ch, miss 1 st at base of ch, 10 dc, miss 1 st, 1 dc, turn (11 sts).
Row 28 WS: 1 ch, miss 1 st at base of ch, 8 dc, miss 1 st, 1 dc, turn (9 sts).
Row 29 RS: 1 ch, miss 2 sts at base of ch, 5 dc, miss 1 sts, 1 dc, turn (6 sts).
Row 30 WS: 1 ch, miss 1 st at base of ch, 3 dc, miss 1 st, 1 dc, turn (4 sts).
Fasten off and weave in end.

Left side of the leaf
With RS facing miss the central chain of the leaf and 1 dc, attach yarn in next dc.
Row 23 RS: 1 ch, 16 dc, turn (16 sts).
Row 24 WS: 1 ch, 16 dc, turn (16 sts).
Row 25 RS: 1 ch, miss 1 st at base of ch, 14 dc, dc2inc in last st, turn (16 sts).
Row 26 WS: 1 ch, miss 2 sts, 12 dc, miss 1 st, 1 dc, turn (13 sts).
Row 27 RS: 1 ch, miss 1 st at base of ch, 10 dc, miss 1 st, 1 dc, turn (11 sts).
Row 28 WS: 1 ch, miss 1 st at base of ch, 8 dc, miss 1 st, 1 dc, turn (9 sts).
Row 29 RS: 1 ch, miss 1 st at base of ch, 5 dc, miss 2 sts, 1 dc, turn (6 sts).
Row 30 WS: 1 ch, miss 1 st at base of ch, 3 dc, miss 1 st, 1 dc, turn (4 sts).
Fasten off and weave in end.

Medium leaf
(make 1)

Using 4mm hook and A, ch 2 sts.
Row 1 RS: 3 dc in 2nd ch from hook, turn (3 sts).
Row 2 WS: 1 ch, 1 dc, (1 dc, 1 ch, 1 dc), 1 dc, turn (4 sts).
Row 3 RS: 1 ch, 2 dc, (1 dc, 1 ch, 1 dc) in next ch sp, 2 dc, turn (6 sts).
Row 4 WS: 1 ch, 3 dc, (1 dc, 1 ch, 1 dc) in next ch sp, 3 dc, turn (8 sts).
Row 5 RS: 1 ch, 4 dc, (1 dc, 1 ch, 1 dc) in next ch sp, 4 dc, turn (10 sts).
Row 6 WS: 1 ch, 5 dc, (1 dc, 1 ch, 1 dc) in next ch sp, 5 dc, turn (12 sts).
Row 7 RS: 1 ch, 6 dc, (1 dc, 1 ch, 1 dc) in next ch sp, 6 dc, turn (14 sts).
Row 8 WS: 1 ch, 7 dc, (1 dc, 1 ch, 1 dc) in next ch sp, 7 dc, turn (16 sts).
Row 9 RS: 1 ch, 8 dc, (1 dc, 1 ch, 1 dc) in next ch sp, 8 dc, turn (18 sts).
Row 10 WS: 1 ch, 9 dc, (1 dc, 1 ch, 1 dc) in next ch sp, 9 dc, turn (20 sts).
Row 11 RS: 1 ch, 10 dc, (1 dc, 1 ch, 1 dc) in next ch sp, 10 dc, turn (22 sts).
Row 12 WS: 1 ch, 11 dc, (1 dc, 1 ch, 1 dc) in next ch sp, 11 dc, turn (24 sts).
Row 13 RS: 1 ch, 12 dc, (1 dc, 1 ch, 1 dc) in next ch sp, 12 dc, turn (26 sts).
Row 14 WS: 1 ch, 13 dc, (1 dc, 1 ch, 1 dc) in next ch sp, 13 dc, turn (28 sts).
Row 15 RS: 1 ch, 14 dc, (1 dc, 1 ch, 1 dc) in next ch sp, 14 dc, turn (30 sts).
Row 16 WS: 1 ch, 15 dc, (1 dc, 1 ch, 1 dc) in next ch sp, 15 dc, turn (32 sts).
Row 17 RS: 1 ch, 16 dc, (1 dc, 1 ch, 1 dc) in next ch sp, 16 dc, turn (34 sts).
Row 18 WS: 1 ch, miss st at base of ch, 3 dc, 5 ch, miss 5 dc, dc in next st, 6 dc, (1 dc, 1 ch, 1 dc) in next ch sp, 15 dc, miss 1 st, 1 dc, turn (34 sts).
Row 19 RS: 1 ch, 17 dc, (1 dc, 1 ch, 1 dc) in next ch sp, 17 dc, turn (36 sts).
Row 20 WS: 1 ch, miss st at base of ch, 17 dc, (1 dc, 1 ch, 1 dc) in next ch sp,

16 dc, miss 1 st, 1 dc, turn (36 sts).

Row 21 RS: 1 ch, 6 dc, 4 ch, miss 4 sts, 8 dc (1 dc, 1 ch, 1 dc) in next ch sp, 18 dc, turn (38 sts).

Row 22 WS: 1 ch, miss st at base of ch, 18 dc, (1 dc, 1 ch, 1 dc) in next ch sp, 17 dc, miss 1 st, 1 dc, turn (38 sts).

Row 23 RS: 1 ch, 19 dc, (1 dc, 1 ch, 1 dc) in next ch sp, 19 dc, turn (40 sts).

Row 24 WS: 1 ch, miss st at base of ch, 19 dc, (1 dc, 1 ch, 1 dc) in next ch sp, 18 dc, miss 1 st, 1 dc, turn (40 sts).

Rows 25–26: Rep row 24, twice (40 sts). This will create a straight edge.

You will now work the top of each side of the heart shape separately.

Right side of the leaf

Row 27 RS: 1 ch, 21 dc, turn (21 sts).

Row 28 WS: 1 ch, 19 dc, miss 1 st, 1 dc, turn (20 sts).

Row 29 RS: 1 ch, miss 1 st at base of ch, 19 dc, turn (19 sts).

Row 30 WS: 1 ch, 17 dc, miss 1 st, 1 dc, turn (18 sts).

Row 31 RS: 1 ch, miss 1 st at base of ch, 17 dc, turn (17 sts).

Row 32 WS: 1 ch, miss 1 st at base of ch, 14 dc, miss 1 st, 1 dc, turn (15 sts).

Row 33 RS: 1 ch, miss 1 st at base of ch, 12 dc, miss 1 st, 1 dc, turn (13 sts).

Row 34 WS: 1 ch, miss 1 st at base of ch, 10 dc, miss 1 st, 1 dc, turn (11 sts).

Row 35 RS: 1 ch, miss 1 st at base of ch, 8 dc, miss 1 st, 1 dc, turn (9 sts).

Row 36 WS: 1 ch, miss 1 st at base of ch, 6 dc, miss 1 st, 1 dc, turn (7 sts).

Row 37 RS: 1 ch, miss 1 st at base of ch, 4 dc, miss 1 st, 1 dc, turn (5 sts).
Fasten off and weave in end.

Left side of the leaf

With RS facing miss the central chain of the leaf, attach yarn in next dc.

Row 27 RS: 1 ch, 21 dc, turn (21 sts).

Row 28 WS: 1 ch, miss 1 st at base of ch, 20 dc, turn (20 sts).

Row 29 RS: 1 ch, 18 dc, miss 1 st, 1 dc, turn (19 sts).

Row 30 WS: 1 ch, miss 1 st at base of ch 18 dc, turn (18 sts).

Row 31 RS: 1 ch, 16 dc, miss 1 st, 1 dc, turn (17 sts).

Row 32 WS: 1 ch, miss 1 st at base of ch, 14 dc, miss 1 st, 1 dc, turn (15 sts).

Row 33 RS: 1 ch, miss 1 st at base of ch, 12 dc, miss 1 st, 1 dc, turn (13 sts).

Row 34 WS: 1 ch, miss 1 st at base of ch, 10 dc, miss 1 st, 1 dc, turn (11 sts).

Row 35 RS: 1 ch, miss 1 st at base of ch, 8 dc, miss 1 st, 1 dc, turn (9 sts).

Row 36 WS: 1 ch, miss 1 st at base of ch, 6 dc, miss 1 st, 1 dc, turn (7 sts).

Row 37 RS: 1 ch, miss 1 st at base of ch, 4 dc, miss 1 st, 1 dc, turn (5 sts).
Fasten off and weave in end.

Large leaf (make 2)

Using 4mm hook and A, ch 2 sts.

Row 1 RS: 3 dc in 2nd ch from hook, turn (3 sts).

Row 2 WS: 1 ch, 1 dc, (1 dc, 1 ch, 1 dc), 1 dc, turn (4 sts).

Row 3 RS: 1 ch, 2 dc, (1 dc, 1 ch, 1 dc) in next ch sp, 2 dc, turn (6 sts).

Row 4 WS: 1 ch, 3 dc, (1 dc, 1 ch, 1 dc) in next ch sp, 3 dc, turn (8 sts).

Row 5 RS: 1 ch, 4 dc, (1 dc, 1 ch, 1 dc) in next ch sp, 4 dc, turn (10 sts).

Row 6 WS: 1 ch, 5 dc, (1 dc, 1 ch, 1 dc) in next ch sp, 5 dc, turn (12 sts).

Row 7 RS: 1 ch, 6 dc, (1 dc, 1 ch, 1 dc) in next ch sp, 6 dc, turn (14 sts).

Row 8 WS: 1 ch, 7 dc, (1 dc, 1 ch, 1 dc) in next ch sp, 7 dc, turn (16 sts).

Row 9 RS: 1 ch, 8 dc, (1 dc, 1 ch, 1 dc) in next ch sp, 8 dc, turn (18 sts).

Row 10 WS: 1 ch, 9 dc, (1 dc, 1 ch, 1 dc) in next ch sp, 9 dc, turn (20 sts).

Row 11 RS: 1 ch, 10 dc, (1 dc, 1 ch, 1 dc) in next ch sp, 10 dc, turn (22 sts).

Row 12 WS: 1 ch, 11 dc, (1 dc, 1 ch, 1 dc) in next ch sp, 11 dc, turn (24 sts).

Row 13 RS: 1 ch, 12 dc, (1 dc, 1 ch, 1 dc) in next ch sp, 12 dc, turn (26 sts).

Row 14 WS: 1 ch, 13 dc, (1 dc, 1 ch, 1 dc) in next ch sp, 13 dc, turn (28 sts).

Row 15 RS: 1 ch, 14 dc, (1 dc, 1 ch, 1 dc) in next ch sp, 14 dc, turn (30 sts).

Row 16 WS: 1 ch, 15 dc, (1 dc, 1 ch, 1 dc) in next ch sp, 15 dc, turn (32 sts).

Row 17 RS: 1 ch, 16 dc, (1 dc, 1 ch, 1 dc) in next ch sp, 16 dc, turn (34 sts).

Row 18 WS: 11 ch, miss 9 sts, 8 dc, (1 dc, 1 ch, 1 dc) in next ch sp, 8 dc, 9 ch miss 8 sts, 1 htr, turn (36 sts).

Row 19 RS: 1 ch, 9 dc in ch sp, 9 dc, (1 dc, 1 ch, 1 dc) in next ch sp, 9 dc, 9 dc in ch sp, turn (38 sts).

Row 20 WS: 1 ch, 19 dc, (1 dc, 1 ch, 1 dc) in next ch sp, 19 dc, turn (40 sts).

Row 21 RS: 1 ch, 20 dc, (1 dc, 1 ch, 1 dc) in next ch sp, 20 dc, turn (42 sts).

Row 22 WS: 1 ch, 21 dc, (1 dc, 1 ch, 1 dc) in next ch sp, 21 dc, turn (44 sts).

Row 23 RS: 1 ch, 22 dc, (1 dc, 1 ch, 1 dc) in next ch sp, 22 dc, turn (46 sts).

Row 24 WS: 14 ch, miss 12 sts, 11 dc, (1 dc, 1 ch, 1 dc) in next ch sp, 11 dc, 12 ch, miss 11 sts, 1 htr, turn (48 sts).

Row 25 RS: 1 ch, 12 dc in ch sp, 12 dc, (1 dc, 1 ch, 1 dc) in next ch sp, 12 dc, 12 dc in ch sp, turn (50 sts).

Row 26 WS: 1 ch, 25 dc, (1 dc, 1 ch, 1 dc) in next ch sp, 25 dc, turn (52 sts).

Row 27 RS: 1 ch, 26 dc, (1 dc, 1 ch, 1 dc) in next ch sp, 26 dc, turn (54 sts).

You will now work a couple of short rows to create shape.

Short Row 1 WS: 1 ch, 18 dc, turn,

Short Row 2 RS: 1 ch, miss 1 st, 17 dc, turn.

Row 28: 1 ch, 27 dc, (1 dc, 1 ch, 1 dc) in next ch sp, 27 dc, turn (56 sts).

Short Row 1 RS: 1 ch, 18 dc, turn,

Short Row 2 WS: 1 ch, miss 1 st, 17 dc, turn.

You will now work the top of each side of the leaf separately.

Right side of the leaf

Row 29 RS: 1 ch, miss 2 sts, 5 dc, turn.

Row 30 WS: 1 ch, 5 dc, turn.

Row 31 RS: 1 ch, 5 dc, turn.

Row 32 WS: 1 ch 5 dc, turn.

Row 33 RS: 1 ch, miss 2 sts, 3 dc, 12 ch, miss 10 sts, 10 dc, turn.

Row 34 WS: 1 ch, 10 dc, 10 dc in ch sp, 1 dc, miss 1 st, 1 dc, turn (22 sts).

Row 35 RS: 1 ch, miss 2 sts, 20 dc, turn (20 sts).

Row 36 WS: 1 ch, 20 dc, turn (20 sts).

Row 37 RS: 1 ch, miss 2 sts, 18 dc, turn (18 sts).

Row 38 WS: 1 ch, miss 2 sts, 16 dc, turn (16 sts).

Row 39 RS: 1 ch, miss 2 sts, 11 dc, miss 2 sts, 1 sl st, turn (12 sts).

Row 40 WS: 1 ch, miss 2 sts, 7 dc, miss 2 sts, 1 sl st, turn (8 sts).

Left side of the leaf

Row 29 WS: With WS facing, attach yarn to the right of the leaf edge, 1 ch, miss 2 sts, 5 dc, turn.

Row 30 RS: 1 ch, 5 dc, turn.

Row 31 WS: 1 ch, 5 dc, turn.

Row 32 RS: 1 ch 5 dc, turn.

Row 33 RS: 1 ch, miss 2 sts, 3 dc, 12 ch, miss 10 sts, 10 dc, turn.

Row 34 WS: 1 ch, 10 dc, 10 dc in ch sp, 1 dc, miss 1 st, 1 dc, turn (22 sts).

Row 35 RS: 1 ch, miss 2 sts, 20 dc, turn (20 sts).

Row 36 WS: 1 ch, 20 dc, turn (20 sts).

Row 37 RS: 1 ch, miss 2 sts, 18 dc,

Row 38 WS: 1 ch, miss 2 sts, 16 dc, turn (16 sts).

Row 39 RS: 1 ch, miss 2 sts, 11 dc, miss 2 sts, 1 sl st, turn (12 sts).

Row 40 WS: 1 ch, miss 2 sts, 7 dc, miss 2 sts, 1 sl st, turn (8 sts).

Large stem (make 2)

Using 4mm hook and A, ch 46 sts.

Row 1: 1 dc in 2nd ch from hook, turn (45 sts).

Rows 2–4: 1 ch, 1 dc in each st to end, turn (45 sts).

Fasten off leaving tail of yarn approximately 12in (30cm) long.

Medium stem (make 1)

Using 4mm hook and A, ch 36 sts.

Row 1: 1 dc in 2nd ch from hook, turn (35 sts).

Rows 2–4: 1 ch, 1 dc in each st to end, turn (35 sts).

Fasten off leaving tail of yarn approximately 12in (30cm) long.

Small stem (make 2)

Cut a piece of garden wire 6in (15cm) long. Work chain stitches around the wire. Using A and 4mm hook, place a sl st on your hook. With the wire in your hand that holds your yarn, place the yarn under the wire and your hook over the wire, yarn over the hook and pull through your sl st. Put your hook under the wire and yarn over, pull up, then put your hook over the wire, yarn over, pull through both loops on the hook. Rep until you have covered 4in (10cm) of the wire.

Soil

Using 3.5mm hook and B, make a magic ring (see page 129).

Round 1: 1 ch, 6 dc into the centre of the ring.

Round 2: 2 dc into each st (12 sts).

Round 3: (1 dc, dc2inc) 6 times (18 sts).

Round 4: (2 dc, dc2inc) 6 times (24 sts).

Round 5: (3 dc, dc2inc) 6 times (30 sts).

Round 6: (4 dc, dc2inc) 6 times (36 sts).

Round 7: (5 dc, dc2inc) 6 times (42 sts).

Round 8: (6 dc, dc2inc) 6 times (48 sts).

Round 9: (7 dc, dc2inc) 6 times (54 sts).

Round 10: (8 dc, dc2inc) 6 times (60 sts).

Rounds 11–18: Work 8 rounds straight.

Round 19: (8 dc, dc2tog) 6 times (54 sts).

Round 20: (7 dc, dc2tog) 6 times (48 sts).

Round 21: (6 dc, dc2tog) 6 times (42 sts).

Round 22: (5 dc, dc2tog) 6 times (36 sts).

Round 23: (4 dc, dc2tog) 6 times (30 sts).

Round 24: (3 dc, dc2tog) 6 times (24 sts).

Round 25: (2 dc, dc2tog) 6 times (18 sts).

Stuff firmly with polyester stuffing.

Round 26: (1 dc, dc2tog) 6 times (12 sts).

Round 27: (Dc2tog) 6 times (6 sts).

Using a tapestry needle, weave this yarn through the last dc sts of the round and gather hole together. Fasten off and weave in ends.

Making up

Weave a strand of floristry wire through the centre of the leaves and at the outer edge of each leaf on the wrong side.

Cut two pieces of garden wire about 12in (30cm) long. Cut one plant stake 8in (20cm) long. Place two uncut garden stakes and the cut plant stake in the soil. Take one piece of 12in (30cm)-long garden wire and poke it into the same hole as one of the plant stakes. Slightly bend the wire at the end. Place a large leaf at the end of this wire. Twist the leaf wire around the top of the wire stem. Take a small leaf and its stem and poke this into the same hole as the stake. Then wrap the stem crochet around the stake and wire, encasing all with the crochet. Using the tail of yarn, sew the first and last rows of crochet together. Securely sew the leaves in place. Repeat for the second large and small leaves.

Place the medium leaf at the top of the cut 8in (20cm) plant stake. Twist the wires around the top of the stake. Then wrap the stem crochet around the stem and, using the tail of yarn, sew the first and last rows of crochet together to encase the stem. Securely sew the leaves in place. Manipulate the leaves to create a natural plant shape.

Herringbone Plant

The oval leaves of the herringbone plant are spectacularly variegated with eye-catching red veins running down the centre and branching out in a herringbone pattern. The leaves have the unusual characteristic of lying flat during the day and then closing upwards at night; hence its other common name of prayer plant.

FINISHED SIZE

The plant in its pot is approximately 7in (18cm) tall from the base of the stem to the top of the leaves.

TENSION

Tension is not essential for this project.

YOU WILL NEED

- Hayfield Bonus DK, 100% acrylic (306yd/280m per 100g ball): 1 ball in 699 Lemongrass (A), 698 Ladybird (B), 839 Bottle Green (C) and 947 Chocolate (D)
- 4mm (UK8:USG/6) crochet hook
- 3.5mm (UK9:USE/4) crochet hook
- Polyester stuffing
- Tapestry needle
- 0.35mm floristry wire
- Plant stakes
- Dark green permanent marker pen
- Plant pot approximately 4¾in (12cm) in diameter

Note

Make the stems by encasing plant stakes with crochet. The plant leaves are given their distinctive colouring by using a marker pen to add dark green shading and then slip-stitch surface decoration (see page 135) is added for the red veins. Create strength in the leaf by weaving floristry wire on the underside of the leaf.

Large leaf
(make 3)

Using 4mm hook and A, ch 2 sts.
Row 1 RS: 3 dc in 2nd ch from hook, turn (3 sts).
Row 2 WS: 1 ch, 1 dc, (1 dc, 1 ch, 1 dc), 1 dc, turn (4 sts).
Row 3 RS: 1 ch, 2 dc, (1 dc, 1 ch, 1 dc) in next ch sp, 2 dc, turn (6 sts).
Row 4 WS: 1 ch, 3 dc, (1 dc, 1 ch, 1 dc) in next ch sp, 3 dc, turn (8 sts).
Row 5 RS: 1 ch, 4 dc, (1 dc, 1 ch, 1 dc) in next ch sp, 4 dc, turn (10 sts).
Row 6 WS: 1 ch, 5 dc, (1 dc, 1 ch, 1 dc) in next ch sp, 5 dc, turn (12 sts).
Row 7 RS: 1 ch, 6 dc, (1 dc, 1 ch, 1 dc) in next ch sp, 6 dc, turn (14 sts).
Row 8 WS: 1 ch, 7 dc, (1 dc, 1 ch, 1 dc) in next ch sp, 7 dc, turn (16 sts).
Row 9 RS: 1 ch, 8 dc, (1 dc, 1 ch, 1 dc) in next ch sp, 8 dc, turn (18 sts).
Row 10 WS: 1 ch, 9 dc, (1 dc, 1 ch, 1 dc) in next ch sp, 9 dc, turn (20 sts).
Row 11 RS: 1 ch, 10 dc, (1 dc, 1 ch, 1 dc) in next ch sp, 10 dc, turn (22 sts).
Row 12 WS: 1 ch, 11 dc, (1 dc, 1 ch, 1 dc) in next ch sp, 11 dc, turn (24 sts).
Row 13 RS: 1 ch, miss st at base of ch, 11 dc, (1 dc, 1 ch, 1 dc) in next ch sp, 10 dc, miss 1 st, 1 dc, turn (24 sts).
Rows 14–22: Rep row 13, 9 times (24 sts). This will create a straight edge.
Row 23: 1 ch, miss 2 sts, 10 dc (1 dc, 1 ch, 1 dc) in next ch sp, 9 dc, miss 2 sts, 1 dc, turn (22 sts).
Row 24: 1 ch, miss 2 sts, 9 dc (1 dc, 1 ch, 1 dc) in next ch sp, 8 dc, miss 2 sts, 1 dc, turn (20 sts).
Fasten off and leave a long tail of yarn.

Using the photograph as guide, make shaded lines using the maker pen on the right side of the leaf. Take yarn B and surface slip stitch in the ridge between rows 5 and 6, 9 and 10, 13 and 14, 17 and 18, and 21 and 22. Then surface slip stitch a line down the centre of the leaf. Fasten off and weave in all ends.

Small leaf
(make 6)

Using 4mm hook and A, ch 2 sts.
Row 1 RS: 3 dc in 2nd ch from hook, turn (3 sts).
Row 2 WS: 1 ch, 1 dc, (1 dc, 1 ch, 1 dc), 1 dc, turn (4 sts).
Row 3 RS: 1 ch, 2 dc, (1 dc, 1 ch, 1 dc) in next ch sp, 2 dc, turn (6 sts).
Row 4 WS: 1 ch, 3 dc, (1 dc, 1 ch, 1 dc) in next ch sp, 3 dc, turn (8 sts).
Row 5 RS: 1 ch, 4 dc, (1 dc, 1 ch, 1 dc) in next ch sp, 4 dc, turn (10 sts).
Row 6 WS: 1 ch, 5 dc, (1 dc, 1 ch, 1 dc) in next ch sp, 5 dc, turn (12 sts).
Row 7 RS: 1 ch, 6 dc, (1 dc, 1 ch, 1 dc) in next ch sp, 6 dc, turn (14 sts).
Row 8 WS: 1 ch, 7 dc, (1 dc, 1 ch, 1 dc) in next ch sp, 7 dc, turn (16 sts).

Row 9 RS: 1 ch, 8 dc, (1 dc, 1 ch, 1 dc) in next ch sp, 8 dc, turn (18 sts).
Row 10 WS: 1 ch, miss st at base of ch, 8 dc, (1 dc, 1 ch, 1 dc) in next ch sp, 7 dc, miss 1 st, 1 dc turn (18 sts).
Rows 11–19: Rep row 10, 9 times (18 sts). This will create a straight edge.
Row 20 WS: 1 ch, miss 2 sts, 7 dc (1 dc, 1 ch, 1 dc) in next ch sp, 6 dc, miss 2 sts, 1 dc, turn (16 sts).
Row 21 RS: 1 ch, miss 2 sts, 6 dc (1 dc, 1 ch, 1 dc) in next ch sp, 5 dc, miss 2 sts, 1 dc, turn (14 sts).
Row 22 WS: 1 ch, miss 2 sts, 5 dc (1 dc, 1 ch, 1 dc) in next ch sp, 4 dc, miss 2 sts, 1 dc, turn (12 sts).
Fasten off and leave a long tail of yarn.

Using the photograph as guide, make shaded lines using the maker pen on the right side of the leaf. Take yarn B and surface slip stitch in the ridge between rows 3 and 4, 7 and 8, 11 and 12, and 15 and 16. Then surface slip stitch a line down the centre of the leaf. Fasten off and weave in all ends.

Stem
(make 3)

Using 4mm hook and C, ch 21 sts.

Row 1: 1 dc in 2nd ch from hook, turn (20 sts).

Rows 2–4: 1 ch, 1 dc in each st to end, turn (20 sts). Fasten off leaving a tail of yarn approximately 12in (30cm) long.

Soil

Using 3.5mm hook and D, make a magic ring (see page 129).

Round 1: 1 ch, 6 dc into the centre of the ring.

Round 2: 2 dc into each st (12 sts).

Round 3: (1 dc, dc2inc) 6 times (18 sts).

Round 4: (2 dc, dc2inc) 6 times (24 sts).

Round 5: (3 dc, dc2inc) 6 times (30 sts).

Round 6: (4 dc, dc2inc) 6 times (36 sts).

Round 7: (5 dc, dc2inc) 6 times (42 sts).

Round 8: (6 dc, dc2inc) 6 times (48 sts).

Round 9: (7 dc, dc2inc) 6 times (54 sts).

Round 10: (8 dc, dc2inc) 6 times (60 sts).

Rounds 11–18: Work 8 rounds straight.

Round 19: (8 dc, dc2tog) 6 times (54 sts).

Round 20: (7 dc, dc2tog) 6 times (48 sts).

Round 21: (6 dc, dc2tog) 6 times (42 sts).

Round 22: (5 dc, dc2tog) 6 times (36 sts).

Round 23: (4 dc, dc2tog) 6 times (30 sts).

Round 24: (3 dc, dc2tog) 6 times (24 sts).

Round 25: (2 dc, dc2tog) 6 times (18 sts).

Stuff firmly with polyester stuffing.

Round 26: (1 dc, dc2tog) 6 times (12 sts).

Round 27: (Dc2tog) 6 times (6 sts).

Using a tapestry needle, weave this yarn through the last dc sts of the round and gather hole together. Fasten off and weave in ends.

Making up

Cut pieces of floristry wire approximately 8in (20cm) long for each leaf. Weave a strand of floristry wire through the centre of the leaves on the wrong side. Place the large leaves at the top of the plant stake. Twist the wires around the top of the stake. Push the stakes into the soil so that there is about 4¾in (12cm) remaining above the surface of the soil. Position a small leaf halfway down the stake and another near the base. Twist the leaf wires around the wire stem. Then wrap the stem crochet around the stem and, using the tail of yarn, sew the first and last rows of crochet together to encase the stem. Securely sew the leaves in place. Manipulate the leaves to create a natural plant shape.

〜〜〜〜〜〜

Poinsettia

The glamorous red 'blooms' of the poinsettia are actually leaves. Originally native to Mexico, they have a reputation for being difficult to keep alive and tend to be short-lived, so a woolly version will make a longer-lasting alternative.

FINISHED SIZE

The plant is approximately 8in (20cm) tall.

TENSION

Tension is not essential for this project.

YOU WILL NEED

- Stylecraft Special DK, 100% acrylic, (323yd/295m per 100g ball): 1 ball in 1246 Lipstick (A), 1009 Bottle (B) and 1004 Dark Brown (C)
- Sirdar Happy Cotton, 100% cotton (47yd/43m per 20g ball): Small amount of 788 Quack (D)
- 4mm (UK8:USG/6) crochet hook
- Polyester stuffing
- Tapestry needle
- 0.35mm floristry wire
- 1.2mm garden wire
- Plant pot approximately 4¾in (12cm) in diameter

Note

The petals and leaves are large so you will need to use floristry wire to keep them upright and manipulate them into a natural shape.

Large petal/leaf (make 14)

Make 10 using A and 4 in B.
Using 4mm hook and A, ch 2 sts.
Row 1: 3 dc in 2nd ch from hook, turn (3 sts).
Row 2: 1 ch, dc2inc, 1 dc, dc2inc, turn (5 sts).
Row 3: 1 ch, 1 dc in each st to end, turn (5 sts).

Row 4: 1 ch, dc2inc, 3 dc, dc2inc, turn (7 sts).
Row 5: 1 ch, 1 dc in each st to end, turn (7 sts).
Row 6: 1 ch, dc2inc, 5 dc, dc2inc, turn (9 sts).
Row 7: 1 ch, 1 dc in each st to end, turn (9 sts).
Row 8: 1 ch, dc2inc, 7 dc, dc2inc, turn (11 sts).
Row 9: 1 ch, 1 dc in each st to end, turn (11 sts).
Rows 10–19: Work 10 rows straight, turn (11 sts).
Row 20: 1 ch, dc2tog, 7 dc, dc2tog, turn (9 sts).
Row 21: 1 ch, dc2tog, 5 dc, dc2tog, turn (7 sts).
Row 22: 1 ch, dc2tog, 3 dc, dc2tog, turn (5 sts).
Row 23 RS: Do not fasten off. You will now work around the edge of the petal/leaf working down both sides, 1 ch, 22 dc, 2 ch at tip then work down the second side of the petal/leaf 22 dc. Fasten off and leave a long tail of yarn.

Small petal/leaf (make 4)

Using 4mm hook and A, ch 2 sts.
Row 1: 3 dc in 2nd ch from hook, turn (3 sts).
Row 2: 1 ch, 1 dc in each st to end, turn (3 sts).
Row 3: 1 ch, dc2inc, 1 dc, dc2inc, turn (5 sts).
Row 4: 1 ch, 1 dc in each st to end, turn (5 sts).
Row 5: 1 ch, dc2inc, 3 dc, dc2inc, turn (7 sts).
Rows 6–11: Work 6 rows straight, turn (7 sts).
Row 12: 1 ch, dc2tog, 3 dc, dc2tog, turn (5 sts).
Row 13: 1 ch, dc2tog, 1 dc, dc2tog, turn (3 sts).
Row 14 RS: Do not fasten off. You will now work around the edge of the petal/leaf working down both sides, 1ch, 13 dc, 2 ch at tip then work down the second side of the petal/leaf 13 dc. Fasten off and leave a long tail of yarn.

Stem (make 2)

Using 4mm hook and B, ch 27 sts.
Row 1: 1 dc in 2nd ch from hook, 1 dc in each st to end, turn (26 sts).
Row 2: 1 ch, 1 dc in each st to end, turn (26 sts).
Fasten off leaving a tail of yarn approximately 12in (30cm) long.

Soil

Using 3.5mm hook and C, make a magic ring (see page 129).
Round 1: 1 ch, 6 dc into the centre of the ring.

Round 2: 2 dc into each st (12 sts).

Round 3: (1 dc, dc2inc) 6 times (18 sts).

Round 4: (2 dc, dc2inc) 6 times (24 sts).

Round 5: (3 dc, dc2inc) 6 times (30 sts).

Round 6: (4 dc, dc2inc) 6 times (36 sts).

Round 7: (5 dc, dc2inc) 6 times (42 sts).

Round 8: (6 dc, dc2inc) 6 times (48 sts).

Round 9: (7 dc, dc2inc) 6 times (54 sts).

Round 10: (8 dc, dc2inc) 6 times (60 sts).

Rounds 11–18: Work 8 rounds straight.

Round 19: (8 dc, dc2tog) 6 times (54 sts).

Round 20: (7 dc, dc2tog) 6 times (48 sts).

Round 21: (6 dc, dc2tog) 6 times (42 sts).

Round 22: (5 dc, dc2tog) 6 times (36 sts).

Round 23: (4 dc, dc2tog) 6 times (30 sts).

Round 24: (3 dc, dc2tog) 6 times (24 sts).

Round 25: (2 dc, dc2tog) 6 times (18 sts).

Stuff firmly with polyester stuffing.

Round 26: (1 dc, dc2tog) 6 times (12 sts).

Round 27: (Dc2tog) 6 times (6 sts).

Using a tapestry needle, weave this yarn through the last dc sts of the round and gather hole together. Fasten off and weave in ends.

Making up

On each petal and leaf, use the tail of yarn and a tapestry needle to make small stitches and gather the end of the petal together. Cut 16 pieces of floristry wire approximately 8in (20cm) long. Weave a strand of floristry wire through the centre of the petals and leaves on the wrong side. Arrange the flower petals so that six large red leaves form a star. Then position two small red petals opposite each other on top of the large leaves. Gather the petal wires together on the underside of the flower. Using the tails of yarn, sew the petals together.

Using yarn D, sew five French knots (see page 134) in the centre of the flower.

Cut two pieces of garden wire approximately 10in (25cm) long. Twist the flower petal wires around the top of the wire stem. Position two green leaves opposite each other 2¾in (7cm) from the top of the stem. Twist the leaf wire around the wire stem. Wrap the stem crochet around the stem and, using the tail of yarn, sew the first and last rows of crochet together to encase the stem. Securely sew the leaves in place. Repeat for the second stem.

Poke the end of the wire of each stem through the soil and fold over the wire to secure. Sew the base of the leaf to the top of the soil. Place the two small leaves in the centre and sew them securely in place. Manipulate the petals and leaves to create a natural plant shape.

String of Hearts

This charming houseplant has small heart-shaped leaves with pairs that grow along a trailing vine. I have created the dual colour by having one heart in green and another in purple opposite each other on each strand.

FINISHED SIZE

The longest strands are approximately 8in (20cm) long.

TENSION

Tension is not essential for this project.

YOU WILL NEED

- Scheepjes Sugar Rush, 100% cotton (306yd/280m per 50g ball):
  1 ball in 513 Spring Green (A) and 240 Amethyst (B)
- Scheepjes Merino Soft, 50% wool, 25% microfibre, 25% acrylic (115yd/105m per 50g ball):
  1 ball in 607 Braque (C)
- 2mm (UK14:US–) crochet hook
- 3.5mm (UK9:USE/4) crochet hook
- Polyester stuffing
- Tapestry needle
- Plant pot approximately 2¾in (6cm) in diameter

Note

The top and underside of these leaves have a different colour. You can also use two-colour yarns to naturally create this effect.

Leaf (make 21 in A and 34 in B)

Using 2mm hook, make a magic ring (see page 129).

Row 1: 3 ch, 3 dtr, 3 tr, 1 ch, 1 dtr, 1 ch, 3 tr, 3 dtr, 2 ch, into the centre of the ring, sl st into centre of the ring to fasten off. Fasten off and leave a tail of yarn.

Small vine (make 2)

Using 2mm hook and both A and B together, ch 20 sts.
Fasten off and leave a tail of yarn.

Medium vine (make 3)

Using 2mm hook and both A and B together, ch 30 sts.
Fasten off and leave a tail of yarn.

Large vine (make 2)

Using 2mm hook and both A and B together, ch 40 sts.
Fasten off and leave a tail of yarn.

Soil

Using 3.5mm hook and C, make a magic ring.

Round 1: 1 ch, 6 dc into the centre of the ring.
Round 2: 2 dc into each st (12 sts).
Round 3: (1 dc, dc2inc) 6 times (18 sts).
Round 4: (2 dc, dc2inc) 6 times (24 sts).
Rounds 5–12: Work 8 rounds straight.
Round 13: (2 dc, dc2tog) 6 times (18 sts). Stuff firmly with polyester stuffing.
Round 14: (1 dc, dc2tog) 6 times (12 sts).
Round 15: (Dc2tog) 6 times (6 sts).
Using a tapestry needle, weave this yarn through the last dc sts of the round and gather hole together.
Fasten off and weave in ends.

Making up

Using the tails of yarn, sew the ends of the vines to the centre of the soil. Sew a leaf of B at the end of each vine. Then, after every 10 ch, sew a pair of leaves, 1 in A and another in B opposite each other in the same place. Large vines will have nine leaves, medium vines will have seven leaves and small vines will have five leaves. Sew the remaining leaves in B to the soil directly.

Nephrolepis exaltata

Boston Fern

The Boston fern is an elegant favourite, also called the sword fern. It has graceful, arching fronds with a ruffled appearance that is best displayed using a tweed or slightly variegated yarn to create the crochet leaves.

FINISHED SIZE

The plant in its pot is approximately 6in (15cm) tall and 8in (20cm) wide.

YOU WILL NEED

- Jamieson and Smith 2ply Jumper Weight, 100% wool (126yd/115m per 25g ball):
  1 ball in FC11MIX Green (A)
- Scheepjes Merino Soft, 50% wool, 25% microfibre, 25% acrylic (115yd/105m per 50g ball):
  1 ball in 607 Braque (B)
- 3mm (UK11:US–) crochet hook
- 3.5mm (UK9:USE/4) crochet hook
- Polyester stuffing
- Tapestry needle
- Floristry wire
- Plant pot approximately 4¾in (12cm) pot in diameter

TENSION

Tension is not essential for this project.

Note

The plant leaves are worked in rows. You create strength in the leaf by working around a wire on row 2 (see page 133). You will work one side of the leaf, then the other side.

Small leaf
(make 10)

Row 1: Using 3mm hook and A, ch 17 sts. Hold your floristry wire above your ch sts; you will work around the wire to encase it in the crochet.

Row 2: Insert your hook into the 2nd st from the hook, yarn over the hook, pull through the stitch, put your hook over the wire and the stitches and wrap the yarn over the hook and pull through both loops on the hook, encasing the wire. Rep to the end of the ch stitches, pm, turn (16 sts).
Pull the wire so that it is at the beginning of the row.

Row 3 (First side): Ch 1, 3 sl st, (1 sl st, 4 ch, 1 sl st in 2nd ch, 2 sl st in ch, 1 sl st in foundation ch) twice, (1 sl st, 5 ch, 1 sl st in 2nd ch, 3 sl st in ch, 1 sl st in foundation ch) three times, (1 sl st, 6 ch, 1 sl st in 2nd ch, 4 sl st in ch, 1 sl st in foundation ch) 3 times, (1 sl st, 7 ch, 1 sl st in 2nd ch, 5 sl st in ch, 1 sl st in foundation ch) 3 times (11 fronds).
Now work on the other side of the foundation chain, missing the last 2 ch sts of the foundation ch, work in the opposite side of the last st you worked in.

Row 3 (Second side): (1 sl st, 7 ch, 1 sl st in 2nd ch, 5 sl st in ch, 1 sl st in foundation ch) 3 times, (1 sl st, 6 ch, 1 sl st in 2nd ch, 4 sl st in ch, 1 sl st in foundation ch) 3 times, (1 sl st, 5 ch, 1 sl st in 2nd ch, 3 sl st in ch, 1 sl st in foundation ch) 3 times, (1 sl st, 4 ch, 1 sl st in 2nd ch, 2 sl st in ch, 1 sl st in foundation ch) twice (22 fronds).
Fasten off and weave in ends.

Large leaf
(make 3)

Row 1: Using 3mm hook and A, ch 24 sts. Hold floristry wire above the ch sts; work around it to encase with crochet.

Row 2: Insert the hook into the 2nd st from the hook, yarn over the hook, pull through the stitch, put hook over the wire and the stitches, wrap the yarn over the hook and pull through both loops on the hook, encasing the wire. Rep to the end of the ch stitches, pm, turn (23 sts). Pull the wire so that it is at the beginning of the row.

Row 3 (First side): Ch 1, 3 sl st, (1 sl st, 4 ch, 1 sl st in 2nd ch, 2 sl st in ch, 1 sl st in foundation ch) twice, (1 sl st, 5 ch, 1 sl st in 2nd ch, 3 sl st in ch, 1 sl st in foundation ch) 3 times, (1 sl st, 6 ch, 1 sl st in 2nd ch, 4 sl st in ch, 1 sl st in foundation ch) 3 times, (1 sl st, 7 ch, 1 sl st in 2nd ch, 5 sl st in ch, 1 sl st in foundation ch) 3 times, (1 sl st, 8 ch, 1 sl st in 2nd ch, 6 sl st in ch, 1 sl st in foundation ch) 3 times, (1 sl st, 9 ch, 1 sl st in 2nd ch, 7 sl st in ch, 1 sl st in foundation ch) 4 times (18 fronds).
Now work on the other side of the foundation chain, missing the last 2 ch sts of the foundation ch, work in the opposite side of the last st worked.

Row 3 (Second side): (1 sl st, 9 ch, 1 sl st in 2nd ch, 7 sl st in ch, 1 st in foundation ch) 4 times, (1 sl st, 8 ch, 1 sl st in 2nd ch, 6 sl st in ch, 1 st in foundation ch) 3 times, (1 sl st, 7 ch, 1 sl st in 2nd ch, 5 sl st in ch, 1 st in foundation ch) 3 times, (1 sl st, 6 ch, 1 sl st in 2nd ch, 4 sl st in ch, 1 st in foundation ch) 3 times, (1 sl st, 5 ch, 1 sl st in 2nd ch, 3 sl st in ch, 1 st in foundation ch) 3 times, (1 sl st, 4 ch, 1 sl st in 2nd ch, 2 sl st in ch, 1 st in foundation ch) twice (36 fronds).
Fasten off and weave in ends.

Soil

Using 3.5mm hook and B, make a magic ring (see page 129).

Round 1: 1 ch, 6 dc into the centre of the ring.

Round 2: 2 dc into each st (12 sts).

Round 3: (1 dc, dc2inc) 6 times (18 sts).

Round 4: (2 dc, dc2inc) 6 times (24 sts).

Round 5: (3 dc, dc2inc) 6 times (30 sts).

Round 6: (4 dc, dc2inc) 6 times (36 sts).

Round 7: (5 dc, dc2inc) 6 times (42 sts).

Round 8: (6 dc, dc2inc) 6 times (48 sts).

Round 9: (7 dc, dc2inc) 6 times (54 sts).

Round 10: (8 dc, dc2inc) 6 times (60 sts).

Rounds 11–18: Work 8 rounds straight.

Round 19: (8 dc, dc2tog) 6 times (54 sts).

Round 20: (7 dc, dc2tog) 6 times (48 sts).

Round 21: (6 dc, dc2tog) 6 times (42 sts).

Round 22: (5 dc, dc2tog) 6 times (36 sts).

Round 23: (4 dc, dc2tog) 6 times (30 sts).

Round 24: (3 dc, dc2tog) 6 times (24 sts).

Round 25: (2 dc, dc2tog) 6 times (18 sts).

Stuff firmly with polyester stuffing.

Round 26: (1 dc, dc2tog) 6 times (12 sts).

Round 27: (Dc2tog) 6 times (6 sts).

Using a tapestry needle, weave this yarn through the last dc sts of the round and gather hole together. Fasten off and weave in ends.

Making up

Arrange the three large leaves in the centre of the soil and then place the small leaves around the outside. Poke the wire of each leaf into the soil and then use the long tails of yarn A to sew the base of the leaf securely to the top of the soil. Curl the leaves slightly to create a natural plant shape.

Dionaea muscipula

~~~~~~~~

Venus Flytrap

This is a fascinating specimen; a rare example of a plant that is carnivorous, entrapping insects and arachnids and slowly consuming them. This woolly version is less lethal but still has an attraction of its own.

FINISHED SIZE

The plant is approximately 3½in (9cm) tall.

YOU WILL NEED

- Scheepjes Metropolis, 75% wool, 25% nylon (219yd/200m per 50g ball): 1 ball in 032 Abu Dhabi (A) and 042 Lagos (B)
- Scheepjes Merino Soft, 50% wool, 25% microfibre, 25% acrylic (115yd/105m per 50g ball): 1 ball in 607 Braque (C)
- 3.5mm (UK9:USE/4) crochet hook
- Polyester stuffing
- Tapestry needle
- Floristry wire
- Plant pot approximately 4in (10cm) pot in diameter

TENSION

Tension is not essential for this project.

Note

The plant is worked in spirals using the amigurumi technique (see page 128). Place a marker at the beginning of each round so you know where you are in the pattern.

Small leaf inner (make 3)

Using 3.5mm hook and B make a magic ring (see page 129).

Round 1: 1 ch, 7 dc into the centre of the ring.

Round 2: 2 dc into each st (14 sts).

Round 3: (1 dc, dc2inc) 7 times (21 sts).

Round 4: Work 1 round straight.

Fasten off and leave a long yarn tail.

Small leaf outer (make 3)

Using 3.5mm hook and A make a magic ring.

Round 1: 1 ch, 7 dc into the centre of the ring.

Round 2: 2 dc into each st (14 sts).

Round 3: (1 dc, dc2inc) 7 times (21 sts).

Round 4: Work 1 round straight.

Round 5: Do not fasten off. Place the inner and outer of the leaf with WS together, sl st both sides together through the back loop of each st.

Round 6: *4 ch, sl st into 2nd ch from hook, 1 sl st into next 2 ch, sl st into st at base of ch, 2 sl st; rep from * 10 times. Fasten off and weave in ends.

Large leaf inner (make 5)

Using 3.5mm hook and B make a magic ring.

Round 1: 1 ch, 7 dc into the centre of the ring.

Round 2: 2 dc into each st (14 sts).

Round 3: (1 dc, dc2inc) 7 times (21 sts).

Round 4: (2dc, dc2inc) 7 times (28 sts).

Round 5: Work 1 round straight.

Fasten off and leave a long yarn tail.

Large leaf outer (make 5)

Using 3.5mm hook and A make a magic ring.

Round 1: 1 ch, 7 dc into the centre of the ring.

Round 2: 2 dc into each st (14 sts).

Round 3: (1 dc, dc2inc) 7 times (21 sts).

Round 4: (2dc, dc2inc) 7 times (28 sts).

Round 5: Work 1 round straight.

Round 6: Do not fasten off. Place the inner and outer of the leaf with WS together, sl st both sides together through the back loop of each st.

Round 7: *4 ch, sl st into 2nd ch from hook, 1 sl st into next 2 ch, sl st into st at base of ch, 2 sl st; rep from * 13 times. Fasten off and weave in the ends.

Large stalk (make 5)

Row 1: Using 3.5mm hook and A, ch 15 sts.

Hold your floristry wire above your ch sts; you will work around the wire to encase them in the crochet (see page 133).

Row 2: Insert your hook into the 2nd st from the hook, yarn over the hook, pull through the stitch, put your hook over the wire and the stitches and wrap the yarn over the hook and pull through both loops on the hook, encasing the wire. Rep to the end of the ch stitches. (14 sts).

Pull the wire so that it is at the beginning of the row.

Fasten off and leave a long tail.

Small stalk (make 3)

Row 1: Using 3.5mm hook and A, ch 11 sts.

Hold your floristry wire above your ch sts; you will work around the wire to encase it in the crochet.

Row 2: Insert your hook into the 2nd st from the hook, yarn over the hook, pull through the stitch, put your hook over the wire and the stitches and wrap the yarn over the hook and pull through both loops on the hook, encasing the wire. Rep to the end of the ch stitches. (10 sts).

Pull the wire so that it is at the beginning of the row.

Fasten off and leave a long tail.

Soil

Using 3.5mm hook and C, make a magic ring.

Round 1: 1 ch, 6 dc into the centre of the ring.

Round 2: 2 dc into each st (12 sts).

Round 3: (1 dc, dc2inc) 6 times (18 sts).

Round 4: (2 dc, dc2inc) 6 times (24 sts).

Round 5: (3 dc, dc2inc) 6 times (30 sts).

Round 6: (4 dc, dc2inc) 6 times (36 sts).

Round 7: (5 dc, dc2inc) 6 times (42 sts).

Round 8: (6 dc, dc2inc) 6 times (48 sts).

Rounds 9–16: Work 8 rounds straight.

Round 17: (6 dc, dc2tog) 6 times (42 sts).

Round 18: (5 dc, dc2tog) 6 times (36 sts).

Round 19: (4 dc, dc2tog) 6 times (30 sts).

Round 20: (3 dc, dc2tog) 6 times (24 sts).

Round 21: (2 dc, dc2tog) 6 times (18 sts).

Stuff firmly with polyester stuffing.

Round 22: (1 dc, dc2tog) 6 times (12 sts).

Round 23: (Dc2tog) 6 times (6 sts).

Using a tapestry needle, weave this yarn through the last dc sts of the round and gather hole together. Fasten off and weave in ends.

Making up

Fold each leaf in half and make a few stitches at each end to keep the leaf slightly closed. Then sew one large leaf to the top of a stalk. Push the floristry wire through the centre of the soil and bend the wire over. At the base of the crochet stalk, use the tail of yarn to sew the stalk firmly to the top of the soil. Repeat, sewing the large leaves to the large stalks and the small leaves to small stalks. Make sure each stalk is sewn firmly at its base to the soil.

~~~~~~~~~~~~~~~~~~~~~~~

Moth Orchid

This is a gorgeous houseplant and one that is readily available, but it can be tricky to retain the flowers. By making a crochet version, you can have an everlasting specimen and will never have to see the beautiful flowers drop.

FINISHED SIZE

Plant is approximately 11in (27cm) tall.

YOU WILL NEED

- Sirdar Country Classic 4ply, 50% wool, 50% acrylic (219yd/200m per 50g ball): 1 ball in 967 Forest Green (A) and 954 Chocolate Brown (B)
- Sirdar Snuggly 100% Cotton DK, 100% cotton (116yd/106m per 50g ball): 1 ball in 762 White (C)
- Sirdar Happy Cotton, 100% cotton (47yd/43m per 20g ball): 1 ball in 788 Quack (D), 755 Jammy (E) and 778 Sherbet (F)
- Sirdar Haworth Tweed DK, 50% nylon, 50% wool (180yd/165m per 50g ball): Small amount of 910 Harewood Chestnut (G)
- 3mm (UK11:US–) crochet hook
- 3.5mm (UK9:USE/4) crochet hook
- Polyester stuffing

- Tapestry needle
- 0.35mm floristry wire
- 1.2mm garden wire
- Plant stake
- Orchid clip
- Plant pot approximately 4in (10cm) in diameter

TENSION

Tension is not essential for this project.

Note

The project is worked in spirals using the amigurumi technique (see page 128). Place a marker at the beginning of each round so you know where you are in the pattern.

Leaf
(make 3)

Using 3mm hook and A, make a magic ring (see page 129).

Round 1: 1 ch, 6 dc into the centre of the ring.

Round 2: 2 dc into each st (12 sts).

Round 3: (1 dc, dc2inc) 6 times (18 sts).

Round 4: (2 dc, dc2inc) 6 times (24 sts).

Round 5: (3 dc, dc2inc) 6 times (30 sts).

Rounds 6–15: Work 10 rounds straight.

Round 16: (4 dc, dc2tog) 5 times (25 sts).

Rounds 17–26: Work 10 rounds straight.

Round 27: (3 dc, dc2tog) 5 times (20 sts).

Rounds 28–32: Work 5 rounds straight.

Round 33: (2 dc, dc2tog) 5 times (15 sts).

Fasten off and leave a long tail.

Outer trefoil petals (make 3)

This is the three-petal part of the orchid that forms the back of the flower. You begin the flower working into a round, then each petal is worked forwards and backwards in rows. Using 3.5mm hook and C, make a magic ring.

Round 1: 1 ch, 6 dc into the centre of the ring, join with a sl st.

Petal

Row 1 RS: 1 ch, dc3inc, dc2inc, turn (5 sts).

Row 2 WS: 1 ch 1 dc, (dc2inc) 3 times, 1 dc, turn (8 sts).

Row 3 RS: 3 ch, 1 tr in each st, turn (8 sts).

Row 4 WS: 3 ch, miss st at base of ch, 7 dtr but do not finish off the stitch completely (leave the last loop on the hook; you will have 8 loops on your hook), yarn over, pull through all loops, 2 ch, 1 sl st in first ch, 3 ch, sl st in 3 ch of turning ch on row 3.

Fasten off.

Turn work to RS, attach yarn to next dc on round 1 with a sl st. Rep petal pattern twice. Fasten off and weave in ends.

Two petals (make 3)

This is the two-petal part of the orchid that forms the middle of the flower. You begin the flower working into a round, then each petal is worked forwards and backwards in rows. Using 3.5mm hook and C, make a magic ring.

Round 1: 1 ch, 6 dc into the centre of the ring, join with a sl st.

Round 2: *2 ch, miss 1 dc, 1 dc in next st; rep from * twice.

Petal

Row 1 RS: Sl st into next ch sp, 1 ch, 4 dc, turn (4 sts).

Row 2 WS: 1 ch (dc2inc) 4 times, turn (8 sts).

Row 3 RS: 1 ch, 1 dc in each st, turn (8 sts).

Row 4 WS: 3 ch, miss st at base of ch, 2 dtr in next st, 4 htr, 2 dtr, 1 dtr in last st. Fasten off.

Row 5 RS: Now work around the edge of the petal; attach yarn to the dc before the ch sp of round 2, work 1 dc in the edge of rows 1–3, 2 ch, 1 sl st in the top of each st of row 4, 2 ch and now work 3 dc in the edge of rows 1–3. Fasten off and weave in ends. Attach yarn to next ch sp on round 2 with a sl st. Rep petal pattern. Fasten off and weave in ends.

Inner petals (make 3)

Using 3mm hook and D, make a magic ring.

Round 1: 1 ch, 6 dc into the centre of the ring, join with a sl st.

Fasten off yarn D and leave a long tail of yarn.

Round 2: Attach yarn E with a sl st, *3 ch, 3 tr in next st, 2 ch, miss 1 ch, 1 sl st in next ch, 3 ch, sl st in next st of round 1; rep from * twice.

Fasten off and weave in ends of E.

Bud (make 2)

Using 3mm hook and F, make a magic ring.

Round 1: 3 ch, 7 dtr into the centre of the ring.

Fasten off and leave a long tail of yarn. Using a tapestry needle, weave the yarn through the ends of the stitches and gather together to form a bud.

Stem

Take a strand of wire and work chain stitches around the wire using A and 3mm hook (see page 133). Place a sl st on your hook. With the wire in the hand that holds your yarn, place the yarn under the wire and your hook over the wire, yarn over the hook and pull through your sl st. Put your hook under the wire and yarn over, pull up and put your hook over the wire, yarn over, pull through both loops on the hook. Rep until you have covered the wire as long as you want it for your plant.

Roots (make 3)

Using 3.5mm hook and G, ch 20 sts. Fasten off and leave a long yarn tail. Weave in the other end.

Soil

Using 3mm hook and B, make a magic ring.

Round 1: 1 ch, 6 dc into the centre of the ring.

Round 2: 2 dc into each st (12 sts).

Round 3: (1 dc, dc2inc) 6 times (18 sts).

Round 4: (2 dc, dc2inc) 6 times (24 sts).
Round 5: (3 dc, dc2inc) 6 times (30 sts).
Round 6: (4 dc, dc2inc) 6 times (36 sts).
Round 7: (5 dc, dc2inc) 6 times (42 sts).
Round 8: (6 dc, dc2inc) 6 times (48 sts).
Round 9: (7 dc, dc2inc) 6 times (54 sts).
Round 10: (8 dc, dc2inc) 6 times (60 sts).
Rounds 11–18: Work 8 rounds straight.
Round 19: (8 dc, dc2tog) 6 times (54 sts).
Round 20: (7 dc, dc2tog) 6 times (48 sts).
Round 21: (6 dc, dc2tog) 6 times (42 sts).
Round 22: (5 dc, dc2tog) 6 times (36 sts).
Round 23: (4 dc, dc2tog) 6 times (30 sts).
Round 24: (3 dc, dc2tog) 6 times (24 sts).
Round 25: (2 dc, dc2tog) 6 times (18 sts).

Stuff firmly with polyester stuffing.

Round 26: (1 dc, dc2tog) 6 times (12 sts).
Round 27: (Dc2tog) 6 times (6 sts).

Using a tapestry needle, weave this yarn through the last dc sts of the round and gather hole together. Fasten off and weave in ends.

Making up

Push your covered stem and plant stake through the top of the soil. Attach the flower buds at the other end of the stem. Carefully curve your stem to form an arch. Sew the orchid flowers together, with the inner petals onto the two petals, and sew these on top of the trefoil petals. Once these have been sewn together, sew firmly to the stem. Place a strand of floristry wire inside each of the leaves. Poke the wire into the soil and then sew the base of the leaf securely to the soil. Sew the ends of the roots to the soil. For extra security, attach two small orchid clips to the stem and attach to the stake.

Mountain Cowslip

Striking, colourful and graphic, this plant is valued so much that some people make a special shelf to show off their collection called an 'auricular theatre'. You can create a year-round flowering display by making the stunning crochet version.

FINISHED SIZE

The plant is approximately 5½in (14cm) tall.

YOU WILL NEED

◆ Scheepjes Metropolis, 75% wool, 25% nylon (219yd/200m per 50g ball):
  1 ball in 032 Abu Dhabi (A)
  and 062 Valencia (B)
  Small amount each of 033 Atlanta (C), 078 Lyon (D), 053 Santiago (E) and 042 Lagos (F)
◆ 3mm (UK11:US–) crochet hook
◆ Polyester stuffing
◆ Tapestry needle
◆ Floristry wire
◆ Plant pot approximately 3¼in (8cm) pot

TENSION

Tension is not essential for this project.

Note

The plant leaves are worked in rounds, using the standard amigurumi technique (see page 128). Place a marker at the beginning of each round so you know where you are in the pattern.

of each petal.
Fasten off and weave in all ends.
Arrange the petals so that one
petal edge overlaps the next petal
on one side.

Stems

Cut three strands of floristry wire
approximately 8in (20cm) long. Take a
strand of wire and work chain stitches
around the wire (see page 133) using
A and 3mm hook. Place a sl st on your
hook. With the wire in your hand which
holds your yarn, place the yarn under
the wire and your hook over the wire,
yarn over the hook and pull through
your sl st. Put your hook under the wire
and yarn over, pull up and then put
your hook over the wire, yarn over, pull
through both loops on the hook. Rep
until you have covered two pieces of
wire for 2½in (5cm). Do the same for
the 3rd piece of wire and then, without
fastening off, twist all three pieces
together to form one stem. Encase all
three strands with crochet for a further
2¾in (7cm).

Soil

Using 3mm hook and B, make a
magic ring.
Round 1: 1 ch, 6 dc into the centre of
the ring.
Round 2: 2 dc into each st (12 sts).
Round 3: (1 dc, dc2inc) 6 times (18 sts).
Round 4: (2 dc, dc2inc) 6 times (24 sts).
Round 5: (3 dc, dc2inc) 6 times (30 sts).
Round 6: (4 dc, dc2inc) 6 times (36 sts).
Round 7: (5 dc, dc2inc) 6 times (42 sts).
Round 8: (6 dc, dc2inc) 6 times (48 sts).
Round 9: (7 dc, dc2inc) 6 times (54 sts).
Round 10: (8 dc, dc2inc) 6 times (60 sts).

Leaf
(make 3)

Using 3mm hook and A, make a magic
ring (see page 129).
Round 1: 1 ch, 6 dc into the centre of
the ring (6 sts).
Round 2: (2 dc, dc2inc) twice (8 sts).
Round 3: (3 dc, dc2inc) twice (10 sts).
Round 4: (4 dc, dc2inc) twice (12 sts).
Round 5: (5 dc, dc2inc) twice (14 sts).
Round 6: (6 dc, dc2inc) twice (16 sts).
Round 7: (7 dc, dc2inc) twice (18 sts).
Round 8: (8 dc, dc2inc) twice (20 sts).
Round 9: (9 dc, dc2inc) twice (22 sts).
Round 10: (10 dc, dc2inc) twice (24 sts).
Rounds 11–14: Work 4 rounds straight.
Round 15: (9 dc, dc2tog) twice (20 sts).
Rounds 16–17: Work 2 rounds straight.
Round 18: (8 dc, dc2tog) twice (18 sts).
Rounds 19–20: Work 2 rounds straight.
Round 21: (7 dc, dc2tog) twice (16 sts).
Rounds 22–23: Work 2 rounds straight.

Round 24: (6 dc, dc2tog) twice (14 sts).
Fasten off leaving an 8in (20cm) tail
of yarn.
Flatten leaf.

Flower
(make 3)

Using 3mm hook and C, make a
magic ring.
Round 1: 1 ch, 7 dc into the centre of
the ring. Fasten off yarn C.
Round 2: Change to yarn D, (dc2inc)
7 times (14 sts).
Round 3: (1 dc, dc2inc) 7 times (21 sts).
Fasten off yarn D.
Round 4: Change to yarn E, join with a
sl st to any dc, *(1 htr, 1 tr, 1 dtr, 1 tr, 1 htr)
in next st, 1 sl st in next 2 sts; rep from *
6 times (7 petals). Fasten off yarn E.
Round 5: Change to yarn F, work 1 dc
in the top of each st around the edge

Rounds 11–18: Work 8 rounds straight.
Round 19: (8 dc, dc2tog) 6 times (54 sts).
Round 20: (7 dc, dc2tog) 6 times (48 sts).
Round 21: (6 dc, dc2tog) 6 times (42 sts).
Round 22: (5 dc, dc2tog) 6 times (36 sts).
Round 23: (4 dc, dc2tog) 6 times (30 sts).
Round 24: (3 dc, dc2tog) 6 times (24 sts).
Round 25: (2 dc, dc2tog) 6 times (18 sts).
Stuff firmly with polyester stuffing.
Round 26: (1 dc, dc2tog) 6 times
(12 sts).
Round 27: (Dc2tog)
6 times (6 sts).
Using a tapestry needle,
weave this yarn through
the last dc sts of the round
and gather hole together.
Fasten off and weave in ends.

Making up

Push the covered stem
through the top of the soil.
Attach the flowers at the
top of each of the flower
stems. Place a strand of
floristry wire inside
each of the leaves. Poke
the wire into the soil and
then sew the base of the
leaf securely to the soil.

Gymnocalycium mihanovichii

Red Cap Cactus

This cactus is popular due to its distinctive red cap. It has the alternative common name of the lollipop cactus. This crocheted replica is considerably less spiny than the living version, but still appealingly vibrant in colour.

FINISHED SIZE

The cactus is approximately 4in (10cm) tall and 2in (5cm) in diameter.

TENSION

Tension is not essential for this project.

YOU WILL NEED

- Stylecraft Special DK, 100% acrylic (323yd/295m per 100g ball): Small amount in 1009 Bottle (A), 1246 Lipstick (B) and 1004 Dark Brown (C)
- 3.5mm (UK9:USE/4) crochet hook
- Polyester stuffing
- Tapestry needle
- Plant pot approximately 2¾in (6cm) in diameter

Note

This project is worked in rows. The rib is created by working into the back loop only of each stitch (see page 132).

Cactus

Row 1: Using 3.5mm hook and A, ch 18 sts.

Row 2 WS: 1 tr in 3rd ch from hook, tr into each ch to end, turn (16 sts).

Row 3: Ch 3, tr blo into each st to end, turn (16 sts).

Row 3 forms the pattern. Work a further 14 rows.

With RS together, crochet the first and last rows together:

Next row: Ch1, sl st in every st. Fasten off and leave a long tail.

Cap (make 1)

Row 1: Using 3.5mm hook and B, ch 8 sts.

Row 2 WS: 1 tr in 3rd ch from hook, tr into each ch to end, turn (6 sts).

Row 3: Ch 3, tr blo into each st to end, turn (6 sts).

Row 3 forms the pattern. Work a further 14 rows.

With RS together, crochet the first and last rows together:

Next row: Ch1, sl st in every st. Fasten off and leave a long tail.

Soil

Using 3.5mm hook and C, make a magic ring (see page 129).

Round 1: 1 ch, 6 dc into the centre of the ring.

Round 2: 2 dc into each st (12 sts).

Round 3: (1 dc, dc2inc) 6 times (18 sts).

Round 4: (2 dc, dc2inc) 6 times (24 sts).

Rounds 5–12: Work 8 rounds straight.

Round 13: (2 dc, dc2tog) 6 times (18 sts). Stuff firmly with polyester stuffing.

Round 14: (1 dc, dc2tog) 6 times (12 sts).

Round 15: (Dc2tog) 6 times (6 sts). Using a tapestry needle, weave this yarn through the last dc sts of the round and gather hole together. Fasten off and weave in ends.

Making up

For the cap, along one side seam, sew small running stitches and then gather the end together to form the top of the cap. Firmly stuff the cap, then gather together the stitches of the open end to form a ball. With the cactus, along one side seam, sew small running stitches and then gather the end together to form the top of the cactus. Firmly stuff the cactus. Sew the red cap to the top of the cactus, then sew the open side of the cactus firmly to the soil.

Crochet Know-how

All the information you'll need to create your beautiful crochet plants is explained here. Whether you are a beginner or an expert with crochet, you will discover helpful hints and tips that will bring your woolly foliage to life.

Tools and Materials

The word 'crochet' means 'hook' in French. Unlike knitting, crochet is worked with just one hook, creating a series of connected loops from yarn.

CROCHET HOOKS

Crochet hooks come in a range of materials and sizes. In this book, I use a relatively small range of sizes, between 2mm (UK14:US–) and 4mm (UK8:USG/6). For size 3.5mm (UK9:USE/4) or 4mm (UK8:USG/6), I like to use an ergonomic metal-pointed crochet hook.

YARN

The key issue with crocheting these projects is to find a yarn that replicates the colours and textures of the plants. For example, I love using tinsel yarns to create the look of cactus spines, such as in the Fairy Castle project (see page 36), while I used a mohair blend yarn to recreate the fluffiness of the leaves of the African Violet (see page 16). Many plants look more realistic if you use a tweed yarn with little flecks of contrasting colour, or a variegated yarn with differences in tone, such as with the Curly Jade Plant (see page 52). To recreate the striped patterns of the Tiger Aloe (see page 32), I used a self-striping sock yarn.

STUFFING

Many of the projects require polyester stuffing, for example, for the soil inserts. My preference is Minicraft Supersoft toy stuffing, as this material complies with BS145, BN5852 and EN71 standards and is safe for children. Make sure plants are stuffed so that they are firm but not bulging, as this will distort the look of the overall project.

NEEDLES

You will need a variety of needles for completing the projects, including a tapestry needle for sewing in ends and adding details.

SUPPORTING THE PLANTS WITH STAKES AND CARDBOARD

Real houseplants often benefit from a little support, and this is more the case when your plant is made out of wool. For some of the larger plants such as the Snake Plant (see page 28), or projects that require extra support such as the Moth Orchid (see page 106), I have used plant stakes or bamboo skewers to support the stem. Cut the stick to the right size so that when it is inserted into the pot the plant is placed just below the rim of the pot. The trunk of the Yucca (page 64) is supported with a cardboard tube. The Sweetheart Plant (see page 44) requires a cardboard insert to give some internal structure to the leaves.

SUPPORTING THE PLANTS WITH WIRE

I have used floristry wire and gardening wire in some of these projects, as the leaves and stems often require some support. Several of the projects feature floristry wire being incorporated into the crocheted leaves for internal support, such as the Boston Fern (see page 98), whereas the Inch Plant (see page 68) incorporates wire into the stems. You could also thread a piece of floristry wire down the centre of the leaves on the wrong side, as is done for the Herringbone Plant (see page 86). The thin wire is useful to create a bend in the leaves of your plant and allows you to manipulate them to ensure they look as natural as possible.

You might want to use craft pipe cleaners or chenille-covered wire if you have them at home. Thicker gardening wire is ideal for creating the curve of a stem. In every case, make sure your wire is not poking out of your plant so it does not hurt you or any inquisitive admirer of your work.

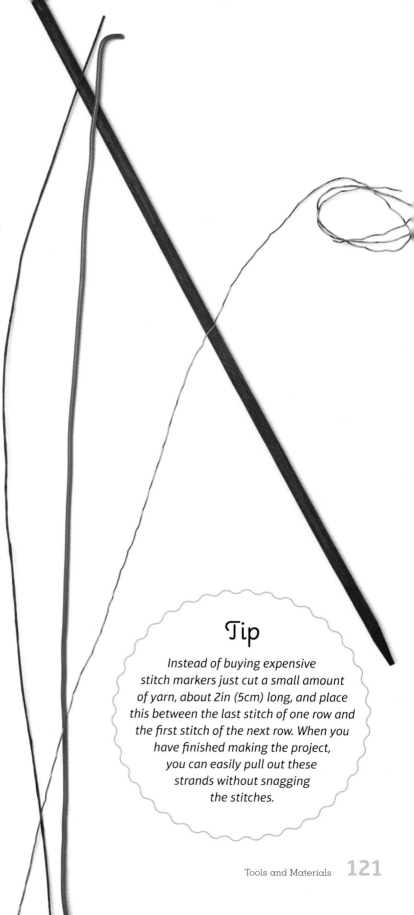

Tip

Instead of buying expensive stitch markers just cut a small amount of yarn, about 2in (5cm) long, and place this between the last stitch of one row and the first stitch of the next row. When you have finished making the project, you can easily pull out these strands without snagging the stitches.

ABBREVIATIONS

alt	alternate
blo	back loop only
ch	chain
ch sp	chain space
cm	centimetres
cont	continue
dc	double crochet
dc2inc	double crochet increase by one stitch
dc2tog	double crochet two stitches together (decrease by one stitch)
dc3tog	double crochet three stitches together (decrease by two stitches)
dec	decrease
DK	double knitting
dtr	double treble
dtr2inc	work 2 dtr into same st
flo	front loop only
g	grams
htr	half treble
htr2inc	work 2 htr into same st
in	inch(es)
inc	increase
m	metre(s)
mm	millimetre(s)
pm	place marker
rep	repeat
RS	right side
RtrF	raised treble front
sl st	slip stitch
sp	space
st(s)	stitch(es)

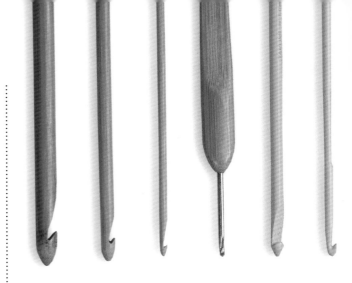

tbl	through the back loop
tog	together
tr	treble
tr2inc	work 2 tr into same st
tr2tog	treble crochet two stitches together (decrease by one stitch)
yd	yard(s)
yo	yarn over
yrh	yarn round hook
WS	wrong side

UK AND US DIFFERENCES

Some UK and US terms have different meanings, which can cause confusion, so always check which style the pattern you are using is written in. This will ensure that your crochet develops correctly.

UK crochet terms	US crochet terms
Double crochet	Single crochet
Half treble	Half double crochet
Treble	Double crochet
Double treble	Triple crochet
Treble treble	Double triple crochet

Note: This book is written in UK crochet terms.

CONVERSIONS

Crochet hook sizes

UK	Metric	US
14	2mm	–
13	2.25mm	B/1
12	2.5mm	–
–	2.75mm	C/2
11	3mm	–
10	3.25mm	D/3
9	3.5mm	E/4
–	3.75mm	F/5
8	4mm	G/6
7	4.5mm	7
6	5mm	H/8
5	5.5mm	I/9
4	6mm	J/10
3	6.5mm	K/10.5
2	7mm	–
0	8mm	L/11
00	9mm	M–N/13
000	10mm	N–P/15

Crochet Techniques

In this section you can learn the basic techniques needed for the projects in this book. Some will need practice, but once you have learnt them you can add texture and decoration to all your crocheted houseplants.

HOLDING A HOOK

Hold your hook in either your right or your left hand as you would a pen, in between your index finger and thumb.

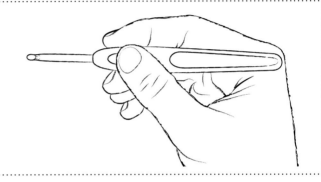

HOLDING YARN

With the hand you are not using to hold the hook, wrap the yarn around your little finger and then drape the yarn over your hand. You can hold the tail of your yarn between the middle finger and your thumb and use your index finger to control the yarn.

MAKING A SLIP KNOT

Make a loop of yarn over two fingers. Pull a second loop through this first loop, pull it up and slip it onto your crochet hook. Pull the knot gently so that it forms a loose knot on the hook.

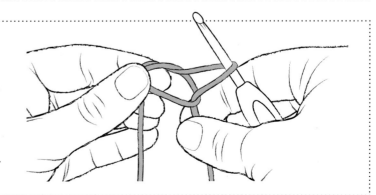

CHAIN STITCH (CH ST)

1   Start with a slip knot on the hook.

2   Wrap the yarn over the hook.

3   Pull the loop through the loop of the slip knot to form one chain stitch.

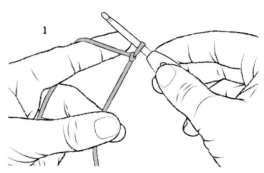

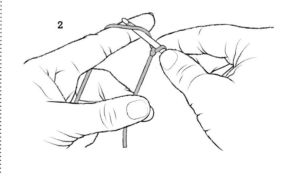

SLIP STITCH (SL ST)

This stitch is ideal for decoration and for attaching two pieces of crochet together.

1   Insert the hook into a stitch, and wrap the yarn over the hook.

2   Draw the loop through the stitch and the loop on the hook. Continue in this way for the required number of slip stitches.

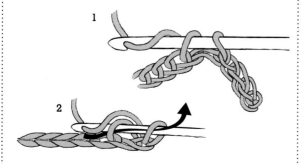

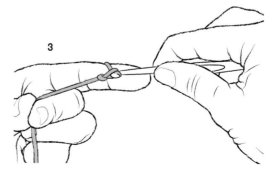

DOUBLE CROCHET (DC)

1 Insert the hook through the stitch, yarn over the hook, and pull through the stitch. There will be two loops on the hook.

2 Wrap the yarn over the hook and pull through both loops on the hook. There will be one loop on the hook.

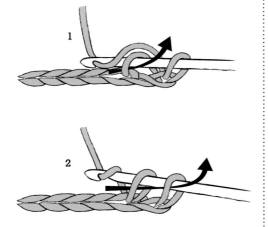

TREBLE CROCHET (TR)

1 Wrap the yarn over the hook, and insert the hook through the stitch. Wrap the yarn over the hook and pull through the stitch

2 Wrap the yarn over the hook and pull through two loops. There will be two loops on the hook.

3 Wrap the yarn over the hook again and pull through the remaining two loops. There will be one loop left on the hook.

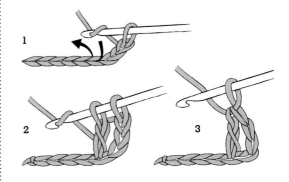

HALF TREBLE (HTR)

1 Wrap the yarn over the hook, insert the hook through the stitch, yarn over the hook and pull through the stitch. There will be three loops on the hook.

2 Wrap the yarn over the hook again and draw through all the loops on the hook. There will be one loop on the hook.

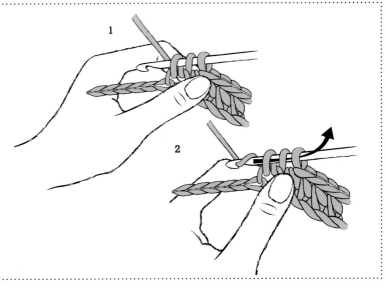

DOUBLE TREBLE (DTR)

1   Wrap the yarn over the hook twice, insert the hook through the stitch, yarn over the hook and pull through the stitch. There will be four loops on the hook

2   Wrap the yarn over the hook and pull through two loops. There will be three loops on the hook.

3   Wrap the yarn over the hook and pull through two loops. There will be two loops on the hook.

4   Wrap the yarn over and pull through the remaining two loops. There will be one loop on the hook.

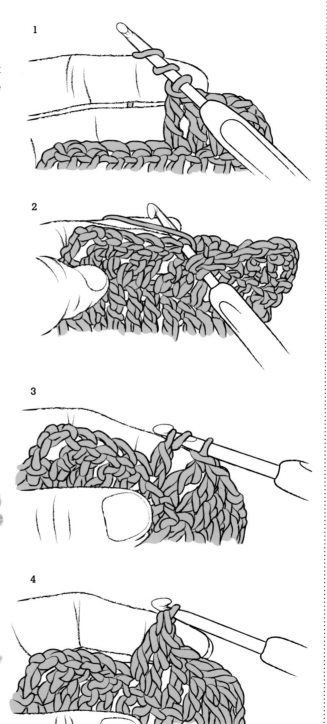

WORKING IN ROWS

When making straight rows, you need to make a turning chain at the beginning of the row for the stitch you are working on. A double crochet row will need one chain at the beginning of the row; this will be indicated in the pattern.

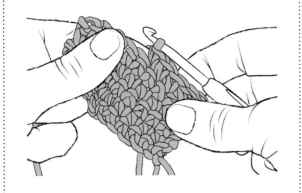

WORKING IN ROUNDS

One wonderful thing about crochet is that you don't always have to work in rows; you can also work in rounds. Many of the patterns in this book are worked in continuous spiral rounds with no slip-stitch joins or turning chains.

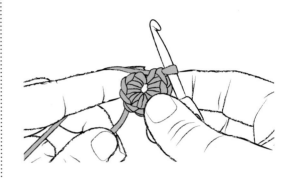

WORKING IN SPIRALS

The majority of the patterns in this book are worked in spiral rounds, beginning with a magic ring. They are worked using the 'amigurumi' crochet technique, which involves crocheting in a continuous spiral with no slip-stitch joins or turning chains. In this way, you can create one seamless cylindrical shape.

In order to know where each row starts it is advisable to place a marker at the beginning of each row.

MAGIC RING

The usual way to start an amigurumi shape is to use a 'magic ring'. This is a neat way of starting a circular piece of crochet while avoiding the unsightly hole that can be left in the centre otherwise. Magic rings are nearly always made with double crochet stitches, as this creates a tight, dense crochet fabric.

1   Start by making a basic slip knot. Pull up the loop and slip this loop onto your crochet hook.

2   Before you tighten the ring, wrap the yarn over the hook (outside the circle) and pull through to make the first chain.

3   Insert the hook into the ring, wrap the yarn over the hook and pull through the ring so there are two loops on the hook.

4   Wrap the yarn over the hook again (outside the circle) and pull through both loops

5   You have made your first double crochet stitch.

6   Continue to work like this for as many double crochet stitches as are stated in the pattern instructions. Pull the yarn tail to tighten the ring and then continue working in the round as usual.

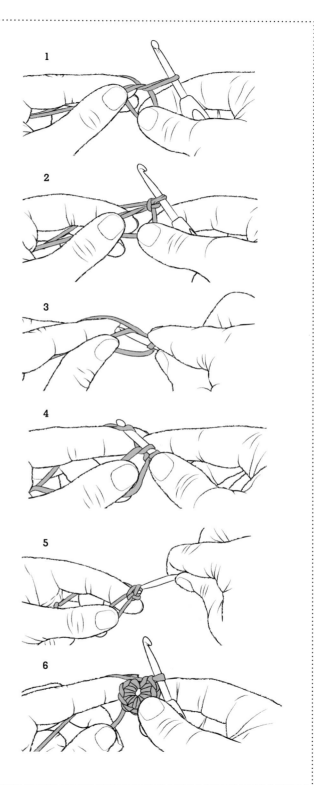

INCREASING (INC)

Work a stitch as normal, then work another one into the same stitch of the previous row.

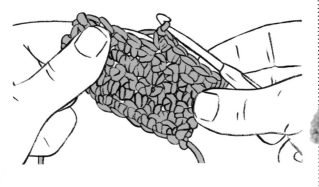

DECREASING (DC2TOG)

1   Insert your hook into the next stitch, pull a loop through, insert your hook into the next stitch, and pull a loop through.

2   Wrap the yarn over the hook and pull the yarn through all three loops.

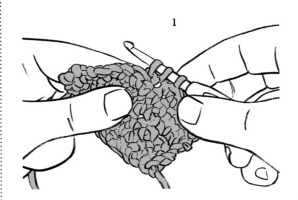

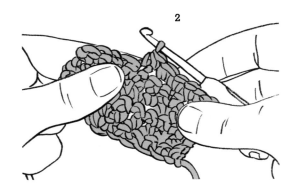

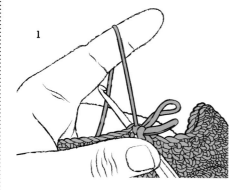

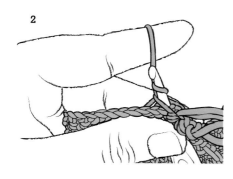

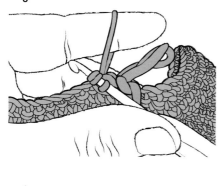

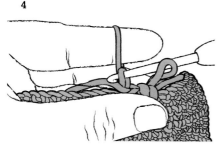

LOOP STITCH

The leaves of the Donkey's Tail (see page 48) are created by creating a loop of yarn.

1   Attach the yarn to the surface of the crochet using a slip stitch. With the yarn over your index finger, put the hook into your stitch.

2   Catch the yarn at the back of the finger and at the front of your finger.

3   Pull through to the front of the stitch, yarn over again and pull through all the stitches on your hook.

4   Remove your finger and begin again with the yarn over your index finger to start the next stitch. This will create a series of loops on the surface of your crochet.

PUFF STITCH

The Crown Cactus pattern (see page 76) creates a puff by drawing several loops together and then making a sl st in the first ch of the stitch.

1   Yarn over hook, insert hook into next st.

2   Yarn over and draw the loop through to the height of 2 ch sts.

3   Rep twice into the same st. You will have 7 loops on your hook. Yarn over and draw through all loops on hook. Make 1 ch st to secure.

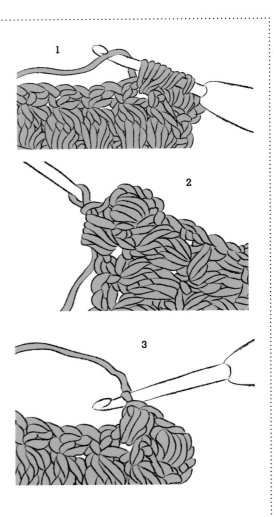

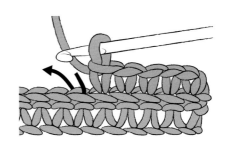

WORKING IN THE BACK LOOP

Generally, a crochet stitch is made by slipping the hook under the top two loops of a stitch. You can create a different effect by working into the back loop only (abbreviation: 'blo') of each stitch of one round or row. This creates a ridge or horizontal bar across the row. I have used this technique for several projects in this book, including the Red Cap Cactus (see page 114) and the Fairy Castle (see page 36).

CROCHETING CHAIN STITCHES AROUND WIRE

Several projects in this book feature this technique of incorporating wire into the crochet to add structural integrity to either the stem or the leaves of a plant (for example, the Spider Plant, see page 20). This both stops the project from drooping and allows you to manipulate it once it is complete to create a naturalistic effect when you display it.

1   Place a sl st on your hook. With the wire in the hand that holds your yarn, place the yarn under the wire and your hook over the wire, yarn over the hook and pull through your sl st.

2   Put your hook under the wire and yarn over.

3   Pull up, then put your hook over the wire, yarn over.

4   Pull yarn through both loops on the hook.

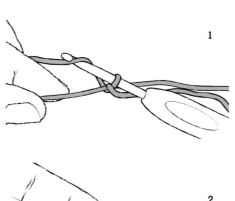

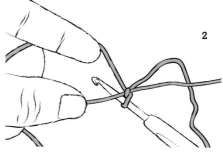

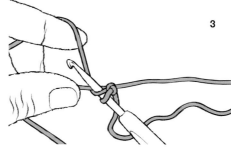

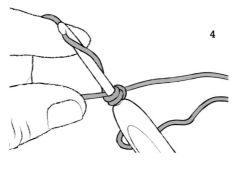

SPIKE STITCH

I used a spike stitch to recreate the leaf pattern of the Coleus (see page 56).

1   Do not work into the next stitch; instead, insert the hook front to back through the top of a stitch one row below.

2   Yarn over and draw a loop through, lengthening the loop to the height of the row being worked, and enclosing the missed stitch.

3   Yarn over and draw through both loops on the hook to complete an elongated double crochet stitch.

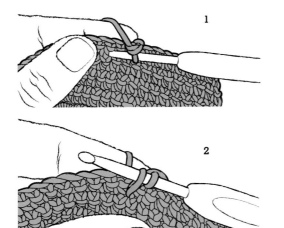

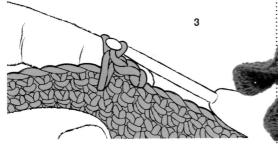

FRENCH KNOT

French knots are ideal for adding dot-like decoration to crochet. I used them for the African Violet (see page 16) and the Poinsettia (see page 90).

1   Bring your needle up through the fabric and then wrap the thread around it three times.
2   Insert the needle back into the fabric very close to where it emerged.

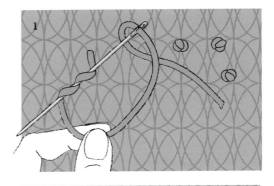

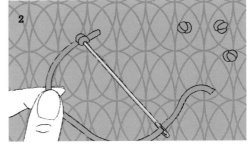

SLIP-STITCH SURFACE DECORATION

You can create a neat line of surface decoration by working a slip stitch between the two rows. This technique is used to add the pattern on the Herringbone Plant (see page 86).

1 Hold the yarn on the wrong side of the fabric and draw a loop up between the stitches.

2 Then push your hook down into the next stitch to hook another loop.

3 Bring this loop up through your first loop to create a chain stitch effect using crochet.

4 To fasten off, cut the yarn and pull through to the front through the last loop. Then, using a tapestry needle, take the yarn back down to the wrong side over the loop, and weave in this end to secure.

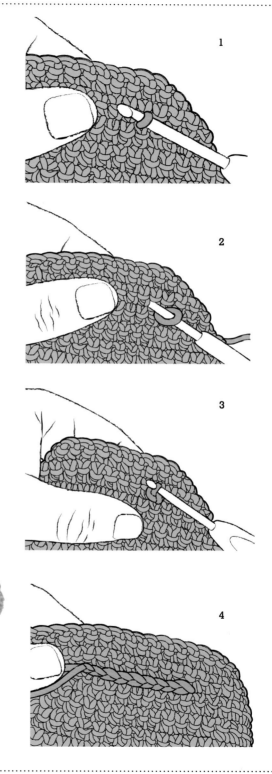

Finishing Off

This section shows you how to make up your project so that it is robust and durable. The type of seams used and the care taken to tidy up messy ends can make a huge difference to the look of the finished plant.

WHIP STITCH

You can use whip stitch to sew two layers of fabric together. Make a knot at the end of your yarn. Bring your needle from the wrong side through to the right side of your fabric, then hold both pieces of your fabric together, wrong sides facing each other. Push your needle from the back piece through to the front piece, and repeat evenly along the edge. There will be a row of small stitches along the edge of your work, joining both pieces together.

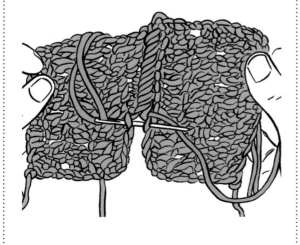

SLIP-STITCH SEAM

Place the pieces of the crochet together with wrong sides facing each other. Insert the hook through both pieces at the beginning of the seam and pull up a loop, then chain one stitch. Work a row of slip stitches by inserting your hook through both sides at the same time.

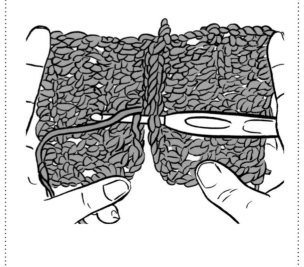

DOUBLE CROCHET SEAMS

Work as for a slip-stitch seam but working double crochet instead of slip stitch. If you work around a corner, work three small stitches into the corners.

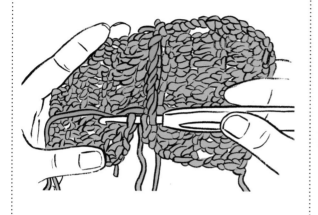

WEAVING IN ENDS

Try to leave about 8in (20cm) of yarn when you fasten off. You may be able to hide the tail in your next row. I always ensure that my ends have been woven backwards and forwards three times.

1 Thread the remaining yarn end onto a tapestry needle and weave in the yarn on the wrong side of the project. Work along the stitches one way, then work back in the opposite direction.

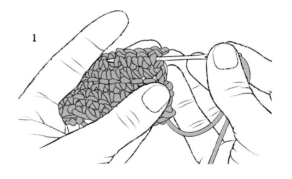

2 Weave the needle behind the first ridge of crochet for at least 2in (5cm). Snip off the end of the yarn close to the fabric of the crochet.

Crocheted Soil

For many of the patterns I chose to make crocheted soil to enhance the display of the project. The aim is to fill your pot with a crocheted sphere made from brown yarn and then stuffed. You can adjust the amount of stuffing in your soil ball to fit your pot. Below are four patterns to suit a range of pot sizes. All of these patterns use a DK-weight wool.

Soil for small pots

This is suited for pots between 2¾in (6cm) and 3in (7cm) in diameter. Using 3.5mm (UK9:USE/4) hook, make a magic ring (see page 129).
Round 1: 1 ch, 6 dc into the centre of the ring.
Round 2: 2 dc into each st (12 sts).
Round 3: (1 dc, dc2inc) 6 times (18 sts).
Round 4: (2 dc, dc2inc) 6 times (24 sts).
Rounds 5–12: Work 8 rounds straight.
Round 13: (2 dc, dc2tog) 6 times (18 sts).
Stuff firmly with polyester stuffing.
Round 14: (1 dc, dc2tog) 6 times (12 sts).
Round 15: (Dc2tog) 6 times (6 sts).
Using a tapestry needle, weave this yarn through the last dc sts of the round and gather hole together. Fasten off and weave in ends.

Soil for medium pots

This is suited for pots between 3¼in (8cm) and 3½in (9cm) in diameter. Using 3.5mm hook, make a magic ring.
Round 1: 1 ch, 6 dc into the centre of the ring.
Round 2: 2 dc into each st (12 sts).
Round 3: (1 dc, dc2inc) 6 times (18 sts).

Round 4: (2 dc, dc2inc) 6 times (24 sts).
Round 5: (3 dc, dc2inc) 6 times (30 sts).
Round 6: (4 dc, dc2inc) 6 times (36 sts).
Rounds 7–14: Work 8 rounds straight.
Round 15: (4 dc, dc2tog) 6 times (30 sts).
Round 16: (3 dc, dc2tog) 6 times (24 sts).
Round 17: (2 dc, dc2tog) 6 times (18 sts).
Stuff firmly with polyester stuffing.
Round 18: (1 dc, dc2tog) 6 times (12 sts).
Round 19: (Dc2tog) 6 times (6 sts).
Using a tapestry needle, weave this yarn through the last dc sts of the round and gather hole together. Fasten off and weave in ends.

Soil for medium-large pots

This is suited for pots between 4in (10cm) and 4¼in (11cm) in diameter. Using 3.5mm hook, make a magic ring.
Round 1: 1 ch, 6 dc into the centre of the ring.
Round 2: 2 dc into each st (12 sts).
Round 3: (1 dc, dc2inc) 6 times (18 sts).
Round 4: (2 dc, dc2inc) 6 times (24 sts).
Round 5: (3 dc, dc2inc) 6 times (30 sts).
Round 6: (4 dc, dc2inc) 6 times (36 sts).
Round 7: (5 dc, dc2inc) 6 times (42 sts).
Round 8: (6 dc, dc2inc) 6 times (48 sts).
Rounds 9–16: Work 8 rounds straight.

Round 17: (6 dc, dc2tog) 6 times (42 sts).
Round 18: (5 dc, dc2tog) 6 times (36 sts).
Round 19: (4 dc, dc2tog) 6 times (30 sts).
Round 20: (3 dc, dc2tog) 6 times (24 sts).
Round 21: (2 dc, dc2tog) 6 times (18 sts).
Stuff firmly with polyester stuffing.
Round 22: (1 dc, dc2tog) 6 times (12 sts).
Round 23: (Dc2tog) 6 times (6 sts).
Using a tapestry needle, weave this yarn through the last dc sts of the round and gather hole together. Fasten off and weave in ends.

Soil for large pots

This is suited for pots between 4¾in (12cm) and 5in (13cm) in diameter. Using 3.5mm hook, make a magic ring.
Round 1: 1 ch, 6 dc into the centre of the ring.
Round 2: 2 dc into each st (12 sts).
Round 3: (1 dc, dc2inc) 6 times (18 sts).
Round 4: (2 dc, dc2inc) 6 times (24 sts).
Round 5: (3 dc, dc2inc) 6 times (30 sts).
Round 6: (4 dc, dc2inc) 6 times (36 sts).
Round 7: (5 dc, dc2inc) 6 times (42 sts).
Round 8: (6 dc, dc2inc) 6 times (48 sts).
Round 9: (7 dc, dc2inc) 6 times (54 sts).
Round 10: (8 dc, dc2inc) 6 times (60 sts).
Rounds 11–18: Work 8 rounds straight.
Round 19: (8 dc, dc2tog) 6 times (54 sts).
Round 20: (7 dc, dc2tog) 6 times (48 sts).
Round 21: (6 dc, dc2tog) 6 times (42 sts).
Round 22: (5 dc, dc2tog) 6 times (36 sts).
Round 23: (4 dc, dc2tog) 6 times (30 sts).
Round 24: (3 dc, dc2tog) 6 times (24 sts).
Round 25: (2 dc, dc2tog) 6 times (18 sts).
Stuff firmly with polyester stuffing.

Round 26: (1 dc, dc2tog) 6 times (12 sts).
Round 27: (Dc2tog) 6 times (6 sts).
Using a tapestry needle, weave this yarn through the last dc sts of the round and gather hole together. Fasten off and weave in the ends.

Note

Finish the soil completely before poking in the stakes and wire. Leave a length of wire or stake free of crochet covering. Wiggle the end into the crochet and through the stuffing and then use a tail of yarn to sew a few small stitches to attach the stem covering to the surface of the soil.

Crocheted Pots

You can source plant pots to display your finished projects, but you could also crochet a pot, and choose any colours you like to complement both the plant and your decor. I find it useful to add some structure by covering a cardboard pot used for seedlings.

FINISHED SIZE

The pot is 2½in (6cm) in diameter at the top and 2in (5cm) in diameter at the bottom. It is 2½in (6cm) high.

YOU WILL NEED

Plain pot

- Stylecraft Life DK, 75% acrylic, 25% wool (326yd/298m per 100g ball): 1 ball in 2448 Bark (A)

Striped pot

- Rico Essentials Cotton DK, 100% cotton (142yd/130m per 50g ball):
  1 ball in 90 Black (A)
  1 ball in 80 White (B)

Funky pot

- Rico Essentials Cotton DK, 100% cotton (142yd/130m per 50g ball):
  1 ball in 14 Fuchsia (A)
  1 ball in 80 White (B)

All pots

- 3mm (UK11:US–) crochet hook
- 1 x biodegradable (cardboard) pot 2½in (6cm) in diameter
- Craft glue

TENSION

Tension is not essential for these projects.

Note

Each pot is worked in spirals using the standard amigurumi technique (see page 128).

Plain pot

Using 3mm (UK11:US–) hook and A, make a magic ring.

Round 1: 1 ch, 8 dc into the centre of the ring.
Round 2: 2 dc into each st (16 sts).
Round 3: (1 dc, dc2inc) 8 times (24 sts).
Rounds 4–5: Work 2 rounds straight.
Round 6: Work 1 round tbl (24 sts).
Round 7: (2 dc, dc2inc) 8 times (32 sts).
Rounds 8–9: Work 2 rounds straight.
Round 10: (3 dc, dc2inc) 8 times (40 sts).
Rounds 11–12: Work 2 rounds straight.
Round 13: (4 dc, dc2inc) 8 times (48 sts).
Rounds 14–18: Work 5 rounds straight.
Rounds 19–20: Work 2 rounds tbl (48 sts).

Fasten off and weave in ends.

Striped pot

Using 3mm (UK11:US–) hook and A, make a magic ring.

Round 1: 1 ch, 8 dc into the centre of the ring.
Round 2: 2 dc into each st (16 sts).
Round 3: (1 dc, dc2inc) 8 times (24 sts).
Rounds 4–5: Work 2 rounds straight.
Round 6: Work 1 round tbl (24 sts).
Round 7: (2 dc, dc2inc) 8 times (32 sts).
Rounds 8–9: Change to B, work 2 rounds straight.
Round 10: Change to A, (3 dc, dc2inc) 8 times (40 sts).
Round 11: Work 1 round straight.
Round 12: Change to B, work 1 round straight.
Round 13: (4 dc, dc2inc) 8 times (48 sts).
Rounds 14–15: Change to A, work 2 rounds straight.
Rounds 16–17: Change to B, work 2 rounds straight.
Round 18: Change to A, work 1 round straight.
Rounds 19–20: Work 2 rounds tbl (48 sts).

Fasten off and weave in ends.

Funky pot

Using 3mm (UK11:US–) hook and A, make a magic ring.

Round 1: 1 ch, 8 dc into the centre of the ring.
Round 2: 2 dc into each st (16 sts).
Round 3: (1 dc, dc2inc) 8 times (24 sts).
Rounds 4–5: Work 2 rounds straight.
In the next row and every following row, work with the two colours, leaving a strand of the colour you are not using just above your work so that it is captured by the yarn you are working.
Round 6: Place a marker at the beginning of each round, (3 dc tbl in A, 3 dc tbl in B) 4 times (24 sts).
Round 7: (3 dc in A, 3 dc in B) 4 times (24 sts).
Round 8: (2 dc, dc2inc in A, 2 dc, dc2inc in B) 4 times (32 sts).
Rounds 9–10: (4 dc in A, 4 dc in B) 4 times (32 sts).
Round 11: (3 dc, dc2inc in A, 3 dc, dc2inc in B) 4 times (40 sts).
Rounds 12–15: (5 dc in A, 5 dc in B) 4 times (40 sts).
Rounds 16–17: Fasten off yarn B and working in A only work 2 rounds straight.
Rounds 18–19: Work 2 rounds tbl (40 sts).

Fasten off and weave in ends.

Making up

Cover the outside of the cardboard pot with some craft glue. Carefully pull the crochet over the pot, making sure the top of the crocheted pot covers the cardboard. Leave to dry.

Acknowledgements

I have always been delighted that so many crafters have enjoyed making my plant projects. For some, it was their entry point into crochet, and so begins a life-long obsession with this incredible craft.

Much of the enjoyment of creating these patterns has been shared with the wonderful team at GMC. They have a passion and dedication to ensure that your craft books are the very best and I am fortunate to work with them. Thank you to my editor Virginia and also to Jonathan Bailey, the publisher who trusts me to come up with appealing projects. Thanks must also go to the wonderful photographer, Andrew Perris, styling by Anna Stevens, illustrations by Martin Woodward and to Lynne Lanning for the overall design. Thank you also to Jude Roust and Nicola Hodgson who did a wonderful job checking everything.

I would like to thank a number of yarn producers and retailers for their support. Thanks to Stylecraft Ltd and the team at Spa Mill, Annabelle and Juliet, who generously donate many of the yarns. Thanks to Sara and the team at Black Sheep Wools for their ongoing support and for being a fab yarn shop.

I continue to love and enjoy the support and encouragement of my crafty best friends Lucy (Attic 24) and Christine (Winwick Mum). You are a joy to my heart.

I am grateful that my family join me in laughing and getting excited by the mad things I create. Benjamin and Robert, I love you.

GMC Publications would like to thank Stupid Egg (stupidegg.co.uk) for the loan of their stunning range of plant pots.

For my favourite nephew Tom Tom

First published 2022 by
Guild of Master Craftsman Publications Ltd
Castle Place, 166 High Street, Lewes,
East Sussex BN7 1XU

Reprinted 2023, 2024

ISBN 978-1-78494-641-8

The publishers and author can accept no legal responsibility
for any consequences arising from the application of
information, advice or instructions given in this publication.

A catalogue record for this book is available from the
British Library.

PUBLISHER Jonathan Bailey
PRODUCTION Jim Bulley
SENIOR PROJECT EDITOR Virginia Brehaut
EDITOR Nicola Hodgson
PATTERN CHECKER Jude Roust
DESIGNER Lynne Lanning
PHOTOGRAPHER Andrew Perris
STYLING Anna Stevens
ILLUSTRATOR Martin Woodward

Colour origination by GMC Reprographics
Printed and bound in Turkey

GMC Publications Ltd
Castle Place, 166 High Street
Lewes, East Sussex
BN7 1XU
United Kingdom
Tel: +44 (0)1273 488005
www.gmcbooks.com